# Spirit Speaks:

## Experiencing Loss of Self

## to Discover Love of Self

by Denise Schaad

# Spirit Speaks

Denise Schaad
Wilseyville, CA
Schaaddenise@gmail.com

Ordering Information:
Special discounts are available on quantity purchases by corporations, associations, educational institutions, and others. For details, contact Denise Schaad above.

Printed in the United States of America
First Edition

ISBN 978-1-5136-9101-5

Publisher: Winsome Entertainment Group LLC

# Part 1

# Trauma Happens

# Chapter 1

# Darkness

*"To know the darkness is to know the Light."*
~Denise Schaad

The white kitchen door with the swinging yellow curtains closes quietly behind me. Mommy holds my hand. We pass the small round kitchen table with its four chairs pushed neatly around it. She calmly leads me by the hand to a small door that's hidden underneath the staircase. She opens the door and tells me that no matter what happens, "Do not come out of the closet." I enter the closet and make my way into the darkness to the very back corner. I notice the shape of the stairs overhead. The floor is wooden, clean, and cold. Nothing is inside the closet except for me and the scary darkness.

As soon as the door closes, my eyes widen. I stare into the darkness, trying to see what is going on. I feel confused and scared. Something is happening outside. Listening intently, I feel my ears are growing bigger. It is quiet, and nothing is moving – I am frozen in fear.

My mind is reeling, feeling loved and nurtured one moment, ending in confusion after being placed in the closet. My heart is pounding in my chest, and I search for other senses to give me clues. I listen.

*Husky male voices I don't recognize are speaking. Mommy is speaking calmly, but I can't hear what she is saying. As the men's voices escalate, I hold my breath, my body stiffens. My eyes widen as if I can see in the dark. Chairs are scraping across the floor. The sound of thumping feet across the kitchen floor is unfamiliar.*

*Listening with my big ears again, I can't hear Mommy. Raspy male voices are becoming louder and louder. I make out that they are looking for my daddy, and she is saying, "I don't know, I don't know." I am frozen, and time stands still until I hear Mommy scream. I cover my ears, and I stifle my scream. My little heart is pumping hard in my chest. Every cry brings a sensation to my entire body. All I can think about is how much I love Mommy. Husky voices are yelling, and I tuck my knees into me so that I won't run out of the closet. I listen with my big ears for Mommy, and finally, I hear her whimpering. I hear stumbling, then a thump, and Mommy screams again. My body tenses.*

*The screaming is so loud I cover my ears; the screaming echoes in my head. My little mind is going crazy. Mommy, Mommy, I scream inside my head. Mommy, my heart throbs for my mommy. All I can think about is my mommy. High alert, knees feel weak, the body goes limp. I collapse to the floor and drift off into another world.*

*As I awaken, the wooden floor feels cold against my cheek. In the darkness, I open my eyes. My heart pounds in my chest, and I can't move. All is silent. I wait and I wait. Then I can't wait any*

4

*longer. But, the last thing my mommy told me was not to come out of the closet. I am five years old and am battling the voices inside my head. She told me to stay in the closet, but I needed to know what was happening outside.*

*I slowly open the door and push the kitchen chairs away to crawl out into the light. The tiny clean kitchen is broken and ransacked. Everything is in chaos. My eyes strain to see what has happened. My feet are cold on the gold shag carpet. The living room is dark except for the light filtering through the drapes. I wander around the room, lost and alone. I find my mommy naked on the floor. I approach her, no response. Crying, I shake her bloody body.*

*"Mommy, Mommy, please wake up."*

*Mommy won't wake up. She's dead!*

*"Mommy, wake up. Please wake up, Mommy, wake up. I will be a good girl. Just wake up, and I will take care of you. Mommy, please wake up. Mommy, please wake up, and I will never leave you. I will always take care of you if you wake up."*

*The front door swings open and I freeze. A man grabs me. I scream for Mommy.*

Even today, fifty years later, it is unclear where I ended up when that man took me away from my mother's side. I have this memory of lying face down on the sidewalk. I trembled within every cell of my body, and I felt my teeth chattering, tears forming,

5

and I was confused and full of terror. I didn't know where I was or how I got there.

I have worked with many energy healers, psychologists, and myself digging into my psyche throughout my spiritual journey. I have this knowing that I ended up in a child prostitution ring. My *knowing* is all I have to go on. Do I need to know the absolute truth? Some things are better left alone. It has taken me a long time to want to know. What I do have is a vision of myself lying on my back. I feel confined, and someone is doing something to me, yet I feel nothing. It is as if I have no connection to my body. I don't know how long I was in the child prostitution ring. But it was long enough for me to decide that no one was ever going to have control over my mind, body, or soul. That day, my mind became my refuge, my illusionary protection from the outside world.

There's a big gap of time that I cannot account for between being taken from my mother's side to that day I was found face down on the sidewalk. When I reunited, it was with my father. My mother was alive, but she also seemed to be missing from that time in my life. I have this sense that she was in a hospital. We never returned to the white stucco house after that day. We moved back to Oakland to an apartment across the street from where I started my first-grade year.

I remember being alone a lot in that apartment, never understanding where my mother was. It was almost like I was alone all the time in my tiny little bedroom that faced the street. Dad was around a little more, but not much. After school, he would be waiting for me on the other side of the crosswalk to walk me home to the apartment. One time, I remember him chasing some colored girls down the street. Like he was protecting me from something.

I don't remember much of the apartment, but my bedroom felt barren, and so did the rest. I don't have a sense of where my five-year-old brother was. But it didn't feel like he was there. It always seemed to be that I was waiting for my mom. Sad and lonely for attention, I would wait for what would seem like hours for my mother to return.

I have this memory of sitting on the floor with my back up against the wall, angrily waiting for my mother to come home. I see myself getting more upset the longer I waited. Darkness would come, fear of the darkness creating more anger that kept me stuck on that cold wooden floor, pissed off that I had to wait so long for my mother.

Eventually my mother came home, most likely from the hospital. The only other memory I have of this apartment was sitting in a kitchen chair in the living room of this upstairs apartment, looking out at my school while my mother fixed my hair for my school picture day. One of my mother's accomplishments in life was going to beauty school. I still have a school picture of myself in a red shirt with no front teeth and this fancy hairdo.

7

## Lost Souls and Secrets

Over the years, Mom would tell stories to me, or I would overhear her telling people about my dad hiding us from the people in his world. The people in the pool hall didn't know my dad had a white wife and two children. Until one day. My mom was suspicious of my dad's infidelity. She got dressed up, went to the pool hall, and announced that she was Joe's wife. They didn't believe her. I think they might have been shocked. My father kept his family a secret from his prostitution and gambling family.

For the first few years of my life, my father served in Vietnam. When he returned, I was about three. My Tia Yolanda gave me a picture of my dad, brother, and me. I am about three years old, dressed in an orange and white polka-dotted dress holding my father's hand, and my brother in a light blue jumpsuit holding his other hand. My dad is wearing gray slacks, and a starched white shirt. He looks handsome and professional. Mom said those were the happy days. The problem, according to her, was that he couldn't behave.

No one ever spoke about that day in the closet. All I have to go on is my knowledge. My mother knew what happened, but she never talked to anyone about being raped. The abuse outside of the closet continued to haunt my family. The violence continued. My mother yelled at my father when he would come home. My father began beating my mother and my brother. And then my mother began to beat me.

Many years later, when my mother got sober, I would find out that she had been raped as a teenager by one of the local boys. She told her parents. Then she was blamed for the rape and sent to live with her sister in Bakersfield. Maybe this was why the rape, during the time I was in the closet, was never mentioned.

It has taken me fifty years to understand the experiences of the memories from my deep dive into my psyche. I have learned that my grandfather and father made a deal with the devil. My grandfather, an immigrant from Mexico, made millions of dollars off prostitution, pornography, and gambling. He owned pool halls and porn shops. At about age nine, my father was living on the streets of Oakland. My grandfather accused my grandmother of having an affair, saying that my father was not his son. My father was not allowed to live in the house with his family. My aunt told me that they would sneak my dad into the house after my grandfather went to sleep. He eventually went to live with his older sister. I share this because my father had that Divine light, but my grandfather didn't like how my father made him feel. So, he got rid of him.

Many years later, I met Joseph, a master healer. His teachings were about how to break soul contracts. Joseph also taught numerology. His numerology teachings about soul agreements showed me that my father was supposed to be the one to free the lineage from the mental and sexual suffering that had enslaved my family and humanity for thousands of years. My father turned to addiction instead. He wasn't able to muster up the courage to do the work.

I have always known that my father was a lost soul. When I learned that his father abandoned him, I understood why. My father served in the Vietnam War as an illegal alien from Mexico. When he returned from the war, my grandfather, who felt guilty, gave him a strip club with a pool hall. My father was twenty-four years old when he mixed up with the wrong people. He started going after other men's women and money. The day I was locked in the closet, it was those people who came to collect their payment or get revenge.

I do recall my mother saying that there was a time when all was perfect in our so-called family life. We lived in the white stucco house with its white picket fence and my mom was happy with her family. My dad returned from Vietnam and inherited the pool hall. He had some money in his pocket.

My mom drove a brand new, 1969 metallic green Chevelle with chrome wheels and red racing stripes on the tires. I remember that car with its black interior and red racing stripes. Mom used to love to drive that car fast down the freeway.

Living in that white two-story stucco house in that quiet neighborhood, we spent a lot of time playing in the backyard with its lush green lawn. I started kindergarten in that neighborhood wearing a blue school uniform. In those days, Mom seemed obsessed with cleaning. She shared with me that her introduction to drugs was diet pills. After having two children in less than two years, my mother was not a thin woman and wanted to look good for my father. She went to a doctor who prescribed diet pills – a legal form of speed.

My mother had never used a drug in her life and probably drank very little alcohol. Unaware that she was on speed, she became obsessed with cleaning the house. I don't think she had anything else to do. She had become a kept woman. Growing up in the city, we stayed clean. I always had a sense mom was there, but I have no memories of her interacting with my brother and me. We had clean clothes and a spotless home. But no interaction with our parents. It always felt like it was just my brother and me. I never remember my dad being there when we lived in that white two-story stucco house in Vallejo.

**Fear: My New Normal**

Fear became my new normal after that day in the closet. My life became one frightening experience after another. Fear haunted my dreams and my everyday life. I had this constant feeling that someone was out to get me. Someone was going to take me and harm me. Someone was going to try and control me.

I have learned about the subconscious programming running in the background of our everyday lives. Meaning the energy surrounds us that's running our thoughts or emotions and feelings. This energy, stored in our emotional body, sits outside our physical body. And these emotional energies run our interactions with our inside world. Soon it is reflected in our outside world. All the while, we believe we have it hidden. These emotions become the secrets that operate our lives.

Fear became lodged in my physical and ethereal bodies. Hence, every interaction with another human being became about reliving that experience. I was reliving the experience unconsciously. Those emotions lodged in my body became the lens through which I viewed myself and this human experience.

After fifteen years of working with a guru, spiritual masters, and energy healers, I now look at everything as a spiritual experience. I mean everything. Nothing ever seems as it appears, and nothing appears as it seems. Every encounter with every human being was a clue to my awakening. Life is a spiritual experience.

I have often wondered who removed me from the sidewalk after the closet incident. There are unseen energies that exist on this planet. Something specific had me hear the call that day. A miracle happened on that day. I am sure that whatever removed me from that experience was not human. I know now from the layers and layers of spiritual work that I've done it is Spirit who has guided and protected me from being enslaved in the child prostitution ring.

My spiritual journey has been more than just unraveling that day in the closet. That day also became the unraveling of the lifetimes of my lineage that has been raping the feminine. I am the one who has chosen to unlock my family's secrets and set them free. What a snake den those secrets turned out to be.

# Chapter 2

# Shadow

*"As long as you don't know yourself, fear will always dictate your life."*
~Anand Mehrotra

*The ringing of the school bell announces the end of the school day. Children hurry to grab their belongings and rush home. Today I am walking home alone. My two-mile walk begins through the township of West Point. Little shops line the two-lane street. I pass by the small general store with all those penny candies that I enjoy so much, especially those little round balls of chocolate, Six-lets. The road meanders upward, and I walk along the old country road that passes by the cemetery.*

*Today I am enjoying my walk home alone. Usually, my brother walks with me, being the little pest that he can be. Today, my mother has taken him to the doctor; he has severe asthma. When his breathing is shallow, it is a struggle for every breath as his chest expands and his little belly sucks in while wheezing sounds come from each exhalation. My brother's already-skinny body became frail when his breathing became restricted. My mother would prop him up on the living room sofa and stay up with him all night. I was afraid for his life. These attacks would come on each spring.*

*The warmth of the sun feels good on my back as I descend the hill. Trees with their new lime green growth catch my attention. Further down the way, the fresh blossoms on the old apple trees smile at me. I notice the happy daffodils as I make my way past Mrs. Porter's green- house. She waves as she does every day. I smile and wave back. I pass the halfway mark of the pond at the tree farm. With its tobacco-colored water, the dampness permeates my nose.*

*I take in the new growth of the fussy cattails prolifically growing along the edges of the pond. I begin the upward climb towards home, breathing the fresh, clean air. I notice the bluebirds flitting to-and-fro in the beautiful blue sky. They seem as happy as I am. The beauty of the spring day fills my heart with gratitude. Independence creates a sense of peace in my belly. From the inside out, I am radiating love. I enjoy every step as I slowly walk up the mile-long hill. I smile as I reach the yellow machine that marks the entrance to my driveway. I am sure that this machine crushed gravel in its day.*

*A sign hangs from the side of the yellow contraption that reads "The Green Barn." Beth and Gena, a lesbian couple, own the Green Barn. The old barn houses treasures from rocks to bones, petrified wood, and antiques. There aren't many kids to play with, so I play in the old barn with all those treasures. Beth and Gena are always kind* and generous to my family and me. I have this sense that they are watching over us.

As I make my way up the gray gravel driveway, I see the fire engine red farmhouse with its white trim that is my home. We are now living in my mother's hometown. My mother, brother, and I have lived here happily for about the last year and a half. At that time, I don't remember my father being around. The three of us have a rhythm that is relaxing and safe. We have times where the three of us laugh at my brother's impression of John Wayne. "Howdy, partner," he says, and mom and I laugh. Mom is laughing again, and I enjoy her being calm. I like living here.

Joyfully, I make my way up to the front door. I glance over at the carport. Mom's light blue nineteen-fifties international pick-up is not there. Delighted with my nine-year-old self, I reach for the round silver knob of the front door. I step into my beautiful, bright, and clean living room with its waxed pine floors. Mom always kept our home tidy during those days. For the past couple of years, Mom nurtured our home, and she was trying to be a good mom. She sewed my dresses, made my cakes, and cooked my breakfast every morning.

Cheerful flowers greet me. Mom has arranged the bouquet of daffodils on top of the buffet that was my grandmother's. My fondest memories with my mother are the two of us picking daffodils from the abandoned house across the road at the driveway's end. To the left of the front door is the staircase that leads up to my bedroom. With my heart open, I make my way up the stairs. To enter my room, I turn left at the top step. A firm hand grabs my arm, shoves me onto the bed, and presses a pillow over my eyes.

Terror fills me. I can't see through the pillow, but it feels like a man. Darkness overtakes me, shocked, confused, stunned. I try to catch my breath. I can't breathe. I can't scream. I hear myself screaming in my head. All I can see are swirling black circles behind my eyes. After that day, those dark swirls haunted me anytime I closed my eyes.

Stunned and shocked, I try to figure out what is happening. A man's sizable, strong hand is pushing the pillow deeper into my face. The other strong hand is tearing at my pants. Thrusting and gripping my legs closed, fighting whoever this is. Rage is coming from this person, the hatred this person has for himself and life. Terrified, I feel heavy darkness coming from him. My anger begins to rise as I fight for my life. I am squeezing and contorting my body in every way possible to keep this human being from entering my sacred place.
Kicking, gripping the pillow with both hands, my rage takes over, and I fight for my life. His penis is inside of me, and wrath and anger are penetrating my sacred place. This man is raping me with a vengeance.

The harder he presses inside of me, the more I leave my body. My mind goes numb. My body goes limp. I have lost the battle of keeping him from penetrating my sacred safe place.

18

*I wake up, and it is dark outside. My teeth are chattering, and I'm cold, and for some reason, I can't move. Numb and confused, I can't move my body. The house is dark and quiet.*


I blocked that memory from my mind, stored it in my body, and lived my life with a closed heart and a sharp mind. I couldn't recall why I was so scared of that room after that day. The darkness I experienced haunted me, and each time I went into that room, I saw those hollow dark circles that reminded me of the devil. And I would hurry up and run downstairs. After that day, I refused to sleep alone. To feel safe enough to sleep, I would negotiate with my brother to let me sleep in the queen-sized bed next to him. Eventually, I moved my bedroom downstairs next to my mother's room.

Soon those dark hollow eye sockets showed up in my third-grade classroom. Those dark circles haunted me when the teacher, Mrs. Landreth put the shade down to block out the afternoon sun. Even with all the confusion inside me, I somehow managed the teacher's strict teachings. I had a desire to learn. I began to withdraw inside myself, trying to control the fear that I felt, that darkness was following me, and I just knew I was a terrible person. I felt the night inside of me. Haunting me but I didn't know why. All I knew was I felt dark and awful. Soon I began overeating until I threw up. It was like I couldn't feel I was full. I was sad and depressed, and I didn't know why. I no longer felt safe at home or in my body. I lived in this constant state of fear that the darkness was going to get me.

Dad just showed up, and he ended up staying with us in that little farmhouse for another year before we got kicked out. Mom became a screaming lunatic. If she wasn't yelling at my father, she was screaming at me. She made us all eat dinner at the yellow table with its chrome legs. It seemed odd that we had to eat at the table with my dad. Mom always stood up and waited on us while we ate. Mom learned to cook Mexican food just how my father liked it when we lived with my Mexican family. Life was no longer calm and relaxing. You never knew when Mom was going to go off the handle. Or when Dad would throw a beer bottle at Mom or punch her in the face because she wouldn't stop bitching at him. It seemed like my mother had it out for my father. I don't think that she was happy to see him again. He was like a putrid stench she couldn't shake.

After that day of having my life force energy altered, I experienced a full year of sore throats. I shut down and hid the secret of being raped deep inside. I felt tormented. I was haunted and felt like a lousy person. But what was strange was I couldn't figure out why I felt so awful about myself.

On that spring day, I went from being in love with my Divine self and all of life to being controlled by fear. It wasn't easy to concentrate at school. Convinced that I was stupid, I kept my mouth shut and didn't speak. I hid from people, and I became invisible and depressed.

I would have no recollection of this memory until I decided to get sober at age thirty-six.

While listening to others speak about their sexual trauma in a drug and alcohol rehab program, a heat began to rise from the depths of my belly, a sharp pull in my gut that signaled the truth of knowing. The realization that sexual abuse had occurred in my life. I was shocked to realize this truth.

When I asked my mother if anything had happened to me as a child, she responded with a stern look on her face. "I tried to keep you safe from him."

I knew it was my dad. But neither one of us could say it.

I hated her at that moment. In not so many kind words, I told her that day that she was a liar and a whore. By her stoic reaction, she knew this day would come.

For the next six months, I went to a therapist weekly and told stories about my mother being the one who sexually abused me. During that time, I never spoke about my father. I could not handle the truth. What I learned about therapy is I am an expert bullshitter. By the end of a session, I had the therapist and myself believing my made-up stories. Therapy was not for me. I needed to find someone to take me deep inside myself to get to the root of my emotions. Eighteen years later I found two energy healers who could take me inward to remember that my father was the one who sexually abused me.

In hindsight, I can see why I hated my mother so much. I hated her each time she allowed my father to come back into our lives. I hated her because she didn't keep us safe from him. I hated her for not allowing me to be happy. My mother was addicted to my father. She hated him as much as she loved him. And this was a dangerous combination for us all.

When he would leave, we would all get a reprieve. Mom would stop yelling and screaming. Our house would be clean, and we could all relax a little. But there was this tension in the background like we were all waiting for that next shoe to drop before she let him back home.

When he showed up, he would be out of money and wanting to clean up his act. He planted himself in the living room chair with a Bible in one hand and a beer in another. He was looking for a way to make himself right. I pretty much stayed away from him. I didn't even talk to him or remember having any interactions with him. He was just there, making us all fearful. It was only a matter of time before he would take off with his paycheck and go and spend it on women and drugs.

My father was addicted to cocaine and women. His infidelity made my mother insane. After that day, I went from feeling connected, open, and free to express my love to sadness. Eventually, I couldn't cope with the sadness, and I became angry. Anger set me on the path of self-hatred toward my inner being and my body. I couldn't understand why I felt so bad about myself. I had begun to live a lie. The lie that I was a horrible person. I had forgotten who I was before being raped. My mind believed I was terrible, and that my thoughts were the truth. I lost connection with my innermost being.

Life became confusing because part of me knew that I was good on the inside. My insides didn't match my thoughts. Life became dark. I lost my connection to my truth and to my ability to express myself. That day I shut down my relationship with my Divine self and began to live the lie of self-deception, fear, anger, and suffering. Stewing in my mad world, I hid my insecurities. I locked up my vagina, my sacred space, from flowing, cutting off the life force flow of energy to my heart. Soon I began to rebel against my parents. I fought with my brother almost daily, beating him up and wrestling him to the ground. Mind you, I outweighed his skinny tiny frame by about twenty pounds.

I felt like I was fighting for that happiness that was there before my father returned. I kept searching for the good in my life. On Sundays, I woke up early, put on a dress, and wore the beige wool coat that my grandmother had given me specifically for going to church. It was my church coat. I recall that the coat came with a gold mouse pin with three little blue topaz stones for the mouse's tail that hung on the coat's collar. My mother hated going to church. She used to say that she spent her childhood going to church two to three times a week, and look where it had gotten her.

I think my mom stopped believing in God somewhere between being raped as a teenager, meeting my dad, and turning to drugs. My father was around my Catholic grandmother, but I don't ever remember him considering church. My brother was never interested in going to church. I snuck out of the house while my parents and brother were still sleeping and walked the mile and a half to church alone. But I always came to the same place in my relationship with God. There was no way in hell I would surrender my will and my life over to God. No way was I going to trust someone or something outside of myself. I would leave church feeling very confused and lonely. I didn't know it then, but I can tell you now that I didn't trust the unclear image of that Father with the long beard who was supposedly God. Why trust and surrender my life to a man that was the one and only Father after the only man I knew as a father had raped me and broken my heart?

Today I know God is me. I am God. God is love. Therefore, I am love. God makes things better. I make things better. Instinctively I knew that what I was searching for was inside of me, not outside of me. There was the intuitive knowing inside of me that was guiding me inward towards myself.

I spent the next forty years going in and out of many churches trying to figure out why anyone would trust and praise a man that was outside of them. I believe that we are brainwashed to believe that God is a man. When you hear the word God, do you automatically think of a man with a beard? That, to me, is an example of mind control. I have searched over the years for God's meaning to me, and I continue to come into clarity about this. It has taken me most of my life to admit that I believe in God. Because of the man thing.

Until I met my second husband, I didn't trust any man. All men became my competition. I felt that I was better than any man. I was out for revenge, but I wasn't aware of it. My intense desire to beat the men fueled my semi-professional mountain bike career. I was out to pass and destroy as many men as I could in each race. There was this personal satisfaction that came when I won races over the men. Training with my first husband was about hammering him on a bike ride and humiliating him in front of his guy friends. I competed in water skiing, triathlons, and cross-country running races to show the men up. In the gym, I would work out and, for my size, outlift them. In my late twenties and early thirties, I was fit and buffed, and no one was going to get near me. If the men looked at me, I would shoot them down with a look of "what the f***."

All the anger was coming from the experience of being raped by my father. I became bitter and angry. Could it be that my pureness made him uncomfortable with his darkness? The energy of my being was love. He misinterpreted this sensual energy as sexual. You see, he was angry with who he had become. He lost sight of his goodness and became dark. I became angry, and the offense became me. Becoming angry kept me locked away from my ability to feel my heart. I separated my soul into my mind, and I buried my spirit deep down in the depths of my heart.

I then turned the anger inward towards myself. My mind hated my life. My spirit loved me. As long as I was angry, I couldn't and wouldn't love me. I became the darkness. The fury now lived inside of me.

By living in the darkness, I created a victim identity. A voice inside telling me I needed to suffer from being part of my family or society. My life became about survival. Survival was all about living from fear and using anger as a weapon against life. Fear has kept me contracted and closed off from expressing my emotions and feeling my feelings. Fear kept me closed off from my heart and spirit. Fear created tension in my body, making it difficult to relax.

To escape the memories and the fear of my parents, I retreated to nature. I played in the trees and the bushes outside the house, building little forts and homes for my dolls and me to feel safe. Outside I was safe from my mother's screaming. The bushes became my friends that kept me hidden from my father's watchful eye. The trees became my guardians who I confided in. I made pathways through the bushes, and this became my fairytale land where everyone got along and was kind to each other.

When the weather turned cold and wet, I created my own tiny home alongside the woodshed. Inside there, I made my fantasy-perfect family. I loved and adored my baby dolls. I would cook on my little stove, and in this imaginary world, my mommy was loving and attentive to her babies. In that tiny little house, the daddy loved and adored his daughter. I enjoyed my unique small home away from the main house. The life I created inside that little shed was free of violence. I found a way to escape my family until the next violent-filled drama happened.

# Chapter 3

# The Choice

*"In the end that was the choice you made, and it doesn't matter how hard it was to make it. It matters that you did."*
~ Cassandra, Clare, Author of **City of Bones**

*I am sitting at the head of the yellow, chrome-legged kitchen table, facing the window. The light in the kitchen streams in from a bank of windows. In front of me sits a two-layer German chocolate cake that my mom made from scratch. My love for chocolate began at an early age. One of the fantastic things about my mother was she could cook. I stare at the candles burning, smiling, and feeling happy.*

*I am turning ten, and this is the first birthday party I ever remember having. Deep down, I wanted this party as I had never wanted anything in my life. I am so happy that my mom has agreed to let me have this party. She stands by the kitchen sink. It's dark in that part of the kitchen. I sense her lurking near me. Her lurking has me feeling uncomfortable, and a part of me feels ashamed that I am the center of attention.*

*I know everyone is singing "Happy Birthday" to me. Yet, in my world, there is no sound. I am staring into the flame of the candles, lost*

29

*in the inability to take it all in. I was happy and scared at the same time. I can't believe I am having this party. I smile and look around me at my fourth-grade closest friends. Shawn and David sit to my right. David is my boyfriend. Ruth, my best friend in the whole world, sits to my left. Susan sits next to her. Each of them has brought me little gifts sitting in front of them wrapped in pretty birthday paper. Mom comes over and slices the cake. I'm afraid of her.*

*I'm so scared she will start one of her yelling sprees. I sit rigid, waiting for her to explode. I know it's coming. I cautiously unwrap each gift, overwhelmed by the uniqueness of each one. I don't know how to respond to the generosity. I feel so embarrassed.*

*Never have this many people at one time been so kind to me. I feel ashamed of all the attention. I go silent and find that place inside my belly that feels safe. Feeling awkward, the party ends, and my friends leave. I'm bewildered by my introverted behavior. I take my gifts and set them atop my dresser for safekeeping. When I return to the kitchen, Mom begins to complain about cleaning up the mess. She starts screaming, and I know what is coming next.*

*I dash across the kitchen and hide under the yellow kitchen table, shocked and confused. My mind instantly has the thought that yellow makes me happy. I like this table. It reminds me of happy times of my family eating together. As dysfunctional as my family was, we always ate our meals together. Her screams turn into a banshee cry.*

*I go deaf and block out her indigenous-sounding voice. Confused and hurt at what is happening, I move to the corner next to the wall. She is trying to get me out from under the table by swinging a metal vacuum cleaner hose.*

*At that moment, I used my anger to overcome my fear of being beaten. It is as if my spirit guides me and gives me the courage to stand up for myself. I come out from under the table to face the wrath of my mother's jealousy. With each blow of the vacuum cleaner hose hitting my back, I stiffen. I will not cry this time. I am taking this without giving my mother the satisfaction of tears. She gets angrier with each blow. I stay silent.*

*In the silence, I feel my rage rising. This sudden anger takes me over. I dig deep. I sense a voice within that sounds like me but different. It speaks to me in a confident tone. My voice is telling me to end these beatings once and for all.*

*I use my anger and self-hatred to stand in that moment and not cry while she hits me with a metal vacuum cleaner hose, over and over again. All the while, I subliminally tell my mother she will never hit me again.*

*At that moment, I knew this would be the last time I would ever take another physical beating from my mother or anyone else for that matter again.*

*She stops swinging, and I slump to the floor holding back my tears of pain and disappointment. I lay on the cold wooden floor. I am ex-*

31

*hausted. I give up the fight for my joy and happiness. That day I stopped fighting for my pleasure. It was too hard to be happy in this family.*

My mother admitted to me that she never wanted the responsibility of having children. She was conflicted with being a mother. Raised by her nine siblings, my mother was the tenth of ten children. She did not get the attention from her mother that she so desperately desired. When my grandmother was dying, my mother finally heard the words *I love you*. She waited all of her life to listen to those three words from her mother. My mother was a child at heart who desired to be loved by that special someone.

As a young child, I was cute and received a lot of attention from my Mexican family. I was the firstborn grandchild, and my grandmother adored me. My mother was twenty with a two-month-old daughter, and she was two months pregnant with my brother. My mother was a white woman living in Oakland with a Mexican family who didn't speak much English. When my father was drafted into the Vietnam war, my mother, brother, and I lived with my Mexican family. My mother was ridiculed and harassed by my uncles. White women are considered second-class citizens to Mexican men. Coming from a small town and Christian upbringing, my mother had to gain street smarts fast. My grandparents made my mother marry my father with their old-fashioned Christian ways once they found out she was pregnant with me.

One day my grandmother said to my mother, "You make your bed. You sleep in it. No matter what, you stay married even if you are miserable and abused."

This statement stuck with me when I had troubles in my first marriage. My mother stayed married to my father for thirty-six years before I convinced her she needed to divorce him. He hadn't been in our lives for over eight years. My brother had unresolved issues with my dad, and he wanted to find him. I made a few phone calls and found out that he had been released from jail and was living in a homeless shelter in Stockton. He had just served a year-long prison sentence for being intoxicated in public one too many times. He was a liability to her. After she divorced him, my father inherited some of my grandfather's fortune, and he gave half of it to her. My father carried a tremendous amount of guilt for what he had done to her and our family.

On my fifty-third birthday, I worked with a woman named Maia, who facilitated psilocybin retreats. During my mushroom experience, I saw that my mother's beatings had a dual meaning: protection and jealousy. Her beatings were about protecting me. I saw that she was trying to beat the light out of me as a way to protect me. My mother thought that she had to protect me, and when she couldn't, it made her angry enough to want to beat me. When I was happy, my light shone, and my true nature shined through. My big heart and compassion vibrated pure love. I can see now that my pure love was sensual and gave others a sense of sexual arousal. Maybe unconsciously, she believed if I hid my light, it would save me from men wanting to have sex with me. The other reason my mother beat me was out of sheer jealousy. That day of my tenth birthday party, my boyfriend had given me a gold necklace. He wanted to show me he cared about me. My mother got scared.

It took a long time to see that my mother was jealous of me. My father's infatuation with me took the attention away from her. As I matured, I would attract a lot of attention. My body was fit, and I took pride in how I looked, and I got a lot of compliments on my body. In some ways, my mother wanted my life.


## The Church's Hold on Sex

Mary Magdalene was perceived as a whore because she had the essence of the sensual energy of the Divine that was mistaken for sex. Everything is a spiritual experience. My journey is about healing the feminine, so this realization made sense. I carry the same kind of energy. My mother mistook it for the whore energy.

The other thing I saw in my healing was that my own mother believed I was a whore. This belief came from the many years she spent in the Baptist Church. My grandparents, her parents, were missionaries from Missouri and helped form the West Point Baptist Church. My mother became a prominent member of the church. She attended Bible study on Wednesdays and taught Sunday school to the children. Funny thing, my mother never spoke to me about religion. I went to church on my own and never considered asking her about God.

The dogma imprinted in her brain had my mother believing that if you liked sex, you were a whore. What is so funny about this is my grandmother had eleven pregnancies. I can remember my mom's oldest sister sharing a story about telling my grandmother that having sex was why she had so many children. Maybe my aunt was having this conversation because she was the one who had to take care of all these babies. Maybe my grandmother didn't know that you could prevent pregnancy, or perhaps she didn't believe in prevention. Either way, my aunt felt the need to let her know having sex created babies. My sense is that sex was not something that my grandmother's generation discussed. It was as if sex was the forbidden conversation in my mother's home. My grandmother did not speak about it if it wasn't in the Bible. The Baptist beliefs go something like this: No dancing. No sex. No fun.

My mother was left to figure out sex on her own. My father was attracted to my mother's church girl innocence. He had never met anyone like her. He had been living on the streets of Oakland since he was nine. He vacationed with his cousins to West Point and met my mother as a teenager. Mother believed that she was born to be an old maid. She truly believed that she was ugly. Meaning, I think she thought that her destiny was to be the one to live at home and take care of her aging

35

parents. When she met my dad, she fell in love with the bad boy image that my father must have exuded.

Her mean brothers confirmed this. When this young, innocent girl got the attention that she had been dying for, she lost her ability to discern and fell head over heels for my father, the handsome Mexican, only to become pregnant soon after. When my father became obsessed with other women, my mother was heartbroken. She couldn't accept that some people got married and were not monogamous.

My mother was pushed over the edge with my father's obsession with me. She couldn't accept it. She turned to harder drugs and alcohol to keep herself numb and hide all the memories of the horrible things that my father put her through. I became the whipping post for her frustrations that she could not vocalize. I took the beatings to make her feel better. I never said anything to her or anyone because I didn't want her to feel bad for beating me. I carried everyone's secrets until I couldn't any longer.

## Behind Closed Doors

There was no more space in my mind or body to hold all my family members' pain and suffering. My anger became displaced towards my mom instead of my dad. I hated her a little more each time she didn't keep me safe. I could not handle the sadness that I felt for not being cared for by my parents. It was easier for me to blame my mother because I blocked my father raping me. But the abuse continued to play out in my family.

My mother hated my father and his shame for being a coward. She was vocal about her hatred towards him. He would come home occasionally, only to get abused by my mother. And my mother would get the beating she felt she deserved from scars of unworthiness that had imprinted on her mind and body from that day in the closet. My father became infatuated with having sex with me. To protect me from my father at night, I pleaded with my brother to sleep in the same bed. Sleeping with my brother frustrated my father. My brother would get regular beatings because he was a good person, but my father could not stand that about him.

The shame I felt for myself, my mother, father, and family stayed behind closed doors. My courage to talk about abuse in my family developed through many years of working on self-actualization. Physical and sexual abuse happen in families more often than not.

I know today that I chose to hide the light of my true nature and disconnect from my heart just a little more. My jaw locked down, and there was no way anyone was going to find out what had happened to me in my own home.

I found myself sad. I moped around and stayed as far away from my mother as possible. I made every excuse not to be at home. I practically lived at my best friend Ruth's house with her family. It was easier for me to be angry at my mother than my father. Her abuse was blatant. My deep sadness was hidden inside my psyche.

I created a fantasy of who my father was because I buried the memory of being raped and wanted to be adored by him. I wanted him to love me and be proud of me. I put my father on a pedestal, and my mother got the wrath of my grief. I know deep down inside she carried a lot of guilt for not protecting my brother and me from my father.

Holding the secrets of my family abuse inside me was taking its toll.

# Chapter 4

# Leaving My Family

*"The only thing that ever dies is the model you have in your mind of who you think you are. That's what dies."*
~Ram Dass

*I'm standing in the dark living room of the mobile home, looking down at my mother sitting on the gold couch with her wounded right leg propped up on throw pillows. Her husky voice from smoking cigarettes and weed is growling at me to clean up the dirty kitchen. When her voice gets like this, I stop listening. I listen to the cedar firewood crackling in the antique cream and greenwood cookstove that used to be my grandmother's.*

*Mom has just returned home from the hospital. She crashed the VW bug while drinking. The old VW gear shift with its missing knob penetrated her right thigh when the vehicle rolled over. She has a deep wound and is unable to walk.*

*Looking over my right shoulder, I see the familiar yellow Formica table with its yellow plastic pads on the seat. A thin white paper plate with a piece of bacon and cubed potatoes sits on the table. This table holds the memories of the four of us who came together as a family.*

*My mother's perspective of mothering was to make our food. I know this was her way of showing us that she loved us. I know that she loves me. Her pain keeps her from being able to express it. I love my mother, I always have.*

*Her DUI is the final straw for me. The dysfunction of taking care of her has taken its toll, and I know it is time for me to choose my well-being over hers. I stop listening to her yelling and make my way to the messy kitchen to heat the water so I can wash the dirty dishes for the last time.*

*I put the kettle on the burner. Pouring soap on the sponge, a knowing inside nudges me. I have to leave my family if I want to graduate high school. Running the hot water into the sink, I scrub a pan. Shame and guilt about abandoning my family overwhelms me. I drop the pan in the sink and go numb.*

*I am eleven and a half, and I have to leave the only family I have ever known if I want to survive. To go, I block out the feelings of love I have for my mother. My heart closes even tighter as I begin to make plans.*

*Drying the pan, I imagine a life where I can take a hot shower, turn on a light switch when it gets dark, and feel comfortable and safe from my father's obsession with me.*

*I walk down the steep rutted, muddy driveway the next day to catch the yellow school bus. I get angrier and angrier with each step as my rubber boots get stuck in the mud. I use the anger to stay numb from the feeling of sadness. I can deal with being angry, but I can't deal with the sadness of having to leave my mother. I know I will not return to that ugly light green mobile home on the hilltop where my family lives. The time had come when it was harder to stay than to leave.*

*I worried about my mother every day. I took on the job to make her happy. Some days I had to motivate her to get out of bed. The truth was by leaving my mother, I disconnected from myself. I blamed myself for her drama-filled life.*

*Riding on the school bus that day, I refused to accept that I deserved to live in a continual state of fear. The only way I knew how to make that happen was to imagine what it would feel like to feel safe somewhere else. I moved in with my boyfriend and his sister Robin, my best friend.*

*I vowed, at that moment, not to be angry with my parents about my choice to leave. I wanted to leave the anger behind and start a new life separate from them. That intuitive voice knew what I needed to hear to move on. It was my way of moving forward into my new life without the family violence.*

*Anger has shown up to motivate me into action when I'm not safe. I become angry when I don't understand what is happening in any given situation. And then, something inside of me awakens and takes over. The innate intuitive part fills with the strength and courage to move forward. Those are the times when something beyond me is guiding me. This decisive energy moves me when my human self can't. I believe this is what it's like to be led by Spirit, and which gave me the courage to leave my family.*


## Safe New Home

Glencoe was nine miles down the canyon across the bridge. That bridge had a hard right turn; driving with too much speed would pull you right into the bridge. Highway 26 twists and turns its way up the canyon. Atop the canyon, right next to the highway, sits a tiny post office, Caltrans station, and the local VFW that make up the township of Glencoe.

I moved to Flying Dove Lane during the spring of my eleventh year on this Earth. I had left my clean but waterless and electricity-less home for this dark, dank depressing home. At least I felt safe. I now lived with my seventeen-year-old boyfriend in his parents' house with forty cats. But I was safe.

The tan two-story house with its brown trim sat off the road, hidden behind a row of cedar trees. The dampness and the coldness that penetrated the house matched the mood of the people who lived here. The front door had twelve little glass panes. The bottom right glass pane missing, allowing only a little light into the dark living room. Heavy gold-colored drapes covered the two other windows in the living room. The smell of cigarettes and cat urine infiltrated my nose as I began to make my way through the dining room to the narrow staircase that led to my new bedroom. The old black steel box in the dining room corner was the only heat source in this cold dark place. On top of the box sat an electric motor that forced the warm air out. The smell of burnt wood would become my new perfume. Cat litter boxes and Persian cats outnumbered the humans by forty to one. This house held many memories over the next twenty-five years: my first marriage, the birth of my two daughters, and all my secrets of addiction.

The first time I met Steve, my best friend Robin's brother, he drove up in his black 1967 VW Bug, his shoulder-length hair parted to one side, wearing a homemade, tie-dyed T-shirt. He gave me that smirk that made his eyes say smart ass. Arrogance covered his insecurity. I mistook this arrogance for confidence: red flag number one. I knew I wanted him to be my boyfriend. It happened quickly, and oh boy was I in for a ride.

I should have known he was trouble when I jumped into that VW with him. He took off with the pedal to the metal, and that little sewing machine was humming down those twisty turning country roads at speeds that invoked the fear of death in me. Thank God he only drove a VW. The faster Steve went, the more smart-ass that smile would get.

We argued from day one – red flag number two. I was used to communicating by yelling at the other person. It was all I knew. When you live in a world where this is all you have learned, you ignore that feeling inside of you that screaming means something is not right here.

It took my mom a few days to come looking for me. When she finally came looking for me, she was met by Steve's dad, Mort, a deputy sheriff. I had told him why I was there and that I wasn't safe at home. My mother would come by every few weeks to see if I had changed my mind. Mort would just tell her, "She doesn't want to go with you." Eventually, she stopped coming. I think because he was a sheriff, she didn't question him.

I don't know how much time went by before I saw her again. I would see my brother at school. I always felt guilty for leaving him to fend for himself. Eventually, I went and visited them in the green mobile home. I would stay long enough to steal some pot and get a little money out of her.

By thirteen, I was using cocaine, pot, or alcohol daily. When I was high, I felt powerful, confident to be seen. Most of all, I was numb. All I knew was that, when I was high, I felt happy. Drugs created this illusion in my mind that I was safe and comfortable.

By sixteen, I found out that I was pregnant. I turned to my mother for help. She made it very clear that there was no way I was going to have a child. I had no other choice but to get an abortion. I was too young to take in the magnitude of how this would affect me later in life. Steve had to come up with the money for the abortion, but I had to go with her because she had to give consent. Afterward, she took me out to lunch as if nothing had happened. I buried the sadness of what I had just done deep inside.

When I left my parents, I made a deal with myself that I would graduate from high school no matter what. I graduated high school three months pregnant. I was sad I had reached my first goal in life, and I couldn't enjoy it. I was pregnant and I was ashamed and disappointed in myself. As much as I tried to make something of myself, I had let myself down.

With the help of a metaphysical healer and Narcotics Anonymous, I was able to find forgiveness for myself. I was able to release myself a little more from the prison of shame and guilt.

## My New Family

In some way, life was still the same. The only difference was instead of being afraid of someone beating me or verbally abusing me, I became even more fearful of being controlled. I had come from a world where my parents' behavior towards me had me believing that there was something wrong with me and that I was not enough.

Over the years, Steve played on my desire to be loved and adored and on my worst fear of being like my mother. He was relentless with his endless criticism and manipulation. I tried to ignore Steve's mental abuse because at least I was safe.

In the spring of my seventeenth year, I found out that I was three months pregnant. The guilt that I carried from my first abortion didn't allow me to consider a second one. Ashley Marie was born on December 16, 1983. She had blonde hair and blue eyes that stared back at me as I held this tiny human in my arms. I loved her, yet I was scared and utterly unaware of how to take care of a child. I was eighteen. I needed my mother.

Jessica Lynn was born two years and two days later, on December 18, 1985, with thick curly brown hair and the most beautiful brown eyes. Out of all my pregnancies, this one was planned. I wanted Ashley to have a sibling. My mom was there with me when I gave birth to both of my daughters. She became a big part of raising my kids. They have memories of getting grandma to sit in their playhouse outside all day as long as they kept bringing her beer. She was there for them when I couldn't be. They both have the fondest memories of her.

By the time I was twenty, I had a two-year-old and a six-month-old daughter, and I got my first job working at an industrial laundry. I instinctively knew that I needed to have my own money. That money gave me freedom. I knew that there was no way I was going to be stuck in a relationship with a man because of a lack of funds. Having children and a job woke me up to my drug use. I soon replaced the sense of control the drugs gave me with an obsession with exercise, the appearance of my body, and making money. The fitter and happier I became, the more Steve tried to break me down.

Steve was always trying to get me to do things his way: hand over my money, take care of the kids, clean the house, cook, shop, do the yard work, go to the dump, put up with him selling drugs instead of getting a job, and oh yes, agree to have an open marriage.

If I resisted him or asked him to participate in any of the mundane chores of life, he became angry and yelled over me. In his loud, angry voice, he would say things like: "You think you're better than me, don't you?"

"You are just like your mother, stupid and lazy."

"No matter what you do, you are only going to end up a no good nothing."

"It doesn't matter how good you look; you're still going to be stupid."

"It doesn't matter how much money you make; you are still going to need me."

"You are nothing without me and never will amount to anything more than a worthless drug addict like your mother."

His agitated, explosive words left me doubting the very essence of my being and left me feeling unlovable. When I didn't fight back, his mouth would continue on a mile a minute, loudly speaking over and at me. He rattled my brain until I was convinced that I was not enough and that my desire for love and happiness caused me to give in to his demands.

Feeling ashamed and guilty, I caved in and gave him what he wanted. Of course, his wanting to have sex with other women was my fault because I wasn't good enough in bed for him. At least when he was with the other women, I wasn't the focus of his defaults.

Exercise became my new drug. Steve couldn't make me feel guilty for exercising and making money. I had found a way to escape his manipulation through training and working forty hours a week. By now, I was gaining confidence through my physical addiction, financial freedom, and he felt threatened. He couldn't handle the amount of attention I received. His mind games were no longer working to his advantage. I was in control now.

When the kids got older, I bought a bicycle. That bicycle turned into a semi-professional mountain biking career. Mountain biking gave me a way to burn off frustrated energy. I used all my pent-up anger to attack every hill climb. The downhills became about overcoming my fear. Soon I was winning every race. I finally found something that gave me confidence in myself.

The fitter I became, the better my life got. The better I felt, the more women Steve invited into our bed for his pleasure.

The discipline to work forty hours a week and train twenty hours a week kept me clean from the drugs for over ten years. When I quit racing, I lost my focus and outlet to combat Steve's mental abuse. Soon, working, caring for my kids, training, and Steve's infidelity forced me to quit racing after ten years.

Steve's relentless judgments wore me down until I found myself in a cycle of using meth for a few months and then cleaning up for a few months. I felt more confident about myself when I was clean and sober. I was strong when I was sober; I could hold my tongue and not fight. Not fighting back showed Steve that he didn't have power over me. When I wasn't straight, I would argue back, causing him to push up against his addiction. It was as if we were both fighting to keep our secrets secret.

Having sex with my boss' wife about did me in. Sneaking around and hiding his secret addiction to sex was a game for him. He preyed on my fear of being abandoned by having sex with other women. A part of me knew his affairs weren't about me. It was about me not being able to be controlled adequately. He had to have someone to manipulate. He would even go so far as to manipulate our children by telling them that they hadn't seen anyone in the house when he was having sex with other women.

## Escaping Torment

One day I found myself sneaking, lying, and using alcohol and drugs again. I still exercised on top of using. I began to numb myself to the manipulation once again. I think the drugs saved me from his narcissistic programming.

Methamphetamines gave me this coat of armor from the pain and the endless jabber of Steve's criticism. As Steve gained confidence by emotionally and mentally abusing me, he restricted my drug and alcohol use. In his mind, it was OK to be a drug dealer. But he was obsessed with controlling the number of his drugs I could use. He directed my drug use by constantly telling me that I was an addict like my mother. He emotionally abused me, and this made him feel powerful. My drug use gave him something to be righteous about. He harped on my drug use to cover his sex addiction.

But it was harder to deal with Steve's mind games. The more he restricted me, the more I rebelled. Lying and stealing drugs from him became my way of getting back at him. Drugs became my secret obsession to escape his endless mind manipulation. The drugs somehow, I believed in the end, kept me protected from his programming. I didn't care about the marriage anymore.

I left the marriage and my family of seventeen years to save myself. Because he already had another woman, he let me go, but not without a fight for the kids. I was tired of fighting. I gave up full custody to him and trusted in my strong bond with my daughters. That decision, I believe, allowed the girls to see the truth of who he had become. With a conviction in court, Ashley declared that she wanted to be with me at the age of twelve. I obtained fifty-fifty custody of the girls.

Over the next six months, I struggled to get out of bed and go to work. I was strung out from the drugs and emotionally and physically spent. I spent the first fifteen minutes of each hour at work locked in the bathroom, asleep on the floor. The only way I knew how to get clean and sober was to abstain secretly.

## Narcissism's Hold on My Life

The definition of narcissism, according to an article Timothy J. Legg Ph.D. wrote for Mayo Clinic.org, is a mental condition in which people have an inflated sense of their importance, a deep need for excessive attention, troubled relationships, lack of empathy, fragile self-esteem, vulnerable to the slightest criticism, selfishness (usually extreme) at the expense of others, plus the inability to consider others' feelings at all.

Narcissists lack the skill to make you feel seen, validated, or understood because they don't grasp the concept of feelings. They pick on you constantly and call you names. Their goal is to lower your self-esteem to increase their own because it makes them feel powerful. When you react, it shows them they have the power to affect your emotional state.

Today, when I look back, I believe my parents and Steve were all narcissists. I have learned narcissists are selfish people who are deathly afraid of their own pain, whether mental, physical, emotional, or spiritual. They are unable to recognize the needs of others.

They all attempted to take advantage of me to get what they wanted. My mother's inability to regulate her emotions and behaviors caused her to become depressed and moody. When she fell short of perfection, she became angry. She beat me to gain control over me. I can say that physical violence towards another human being gives narcissistic people the feeling that they are powerful and can control something in their lives. The violence was a cover-up for her lack of self-esteem.

I used to call my father a lost soul. Today I would say he was soulless. Something outside of him was running his thoughts. His acts of sexual violence toward me were to make him feel powerful. His inability to deal with stress or adapt to change created secret feelings of insecurity, shame, and vulnerability that caused him to take it out on others, especially me.

My parents were acting out their pain toward me. I falsely believed their experiences were mine to carry, feel, and transmute. As a sensitive and co-dependent person who wanted to be loved and adored, I took on the mental, emotional, physical, and sexual abuse to unconsciously take on their pain. I've learned that my merging defense was about seeking love and attention because I felt abandoned. By merging my energy with others, I felt connected to them. By joining my energy, it helped me not to feel so alone.

My worst fear is having my thoughts controlled or being controlled by anyone. My will to be a sovereign individual is more vital than anything anyone can do. My mind is strong. I was so strong that, even though I was emotionally, mentally, and physically abused, my Spirit (will) could never surrender to another human being. These experiences kept my ego-mind vigilant.

However, my Spirit has always been there, guiding me towards the light of my true nature. My Spirit helped me move toward my inner truth and the light of my true nature in my fight for sovereignty.

# Part 2

# Healing

# Chapter 5

# Battle Ground for the Truth

*"The most confused we ever get is when we try to convince our heads of something our hearts know is a lie."*
~Karen Moning

Spring had sprung, and oh how I loved springtime. Vibrant green grass, blossoming flowers, and budding trees. The air was fresh and clean. Spring, to me, represented a new beginning. Whether I was aware at the time or not, the Universe was working for me.

I can still see myself sitting in my mother's old one-room cabin at the entrance of the lake road. The little four hundred square foot cabin sat beneath hundred-year-old pine trees. Early on a Tuesday morning, I sat at the old desk covered with a green tablecloth that made it on to my mother's kitchen table. My mother sat across the table from me. Atop the table sat a mirror with lines of meth, two shot glasses of vodka, and a joint in the ashtray.

That day, I was paying attention in-between the lines of meth, the shot of vodka, and the toke of that joint. At seven-thirty in the morning, at thirty-six years of age, I realized that my worst fear had come to fruition. I had become just like my mother, a drug addict and an alcoholic. I had been fooling myself for most of my life that I didn't have these problems. After all, I was an athlete, I had a job, and I drove an expensive car. My life wasn't like my mother's; she lived in a shack on permanent social security, poor, and depressed.

That morning took me by surprise. I was freaked out because my intuition was telling me "You have become your mother." Oh shit! I have a problem, and I don't want to deal with this right now. One more line and another shot, and I will forget what I just heard. But that nagging feeling stayed with me. I tried to get more wired and drunker for the next few weeks to forget it, but I couldn't ignore the bomb my innermost being had dropped on me. "Denise, it's time to stop avoiding yourself."

In reflecting, I have noticed that the most significant events in my life occurred in the spring. In the spring of my senior year in high school, I was pregnant with my first daughter Ashley. It took me a while to get clean, probably another couple of months of using cocaine before fully accepting the pregnancy. Using drugs while I was pregnant has been one of those deep dark secrets that haunted me. Saying this out loud released me from denial.

Ashley was a sweet baby. As a child, she was joyful and loving. I breastfed and carried her in my arms all day long until she was nine months old. Intuitively, I cared for my baby the way I wanted to be cared for by my mother.

Two years later, in the spring of 1985, I was pregnant with my second daughter Jessica. Out of all the pregnancies, this one I planned. I was still using meth off and on then. I began my fixation with exercise to get off the drugs. When I delivered Ashley, I weighed two hundred pounds. I was as wide as I was tall, and I vowed I would never be that heavy again. Pregnant with Jessica, I exercised every day until I was eight months pregnant. I was in labor with Jessica for nineteen hours. Jessica was a pretty easy baby. As a child, she was very intuitive and a little stubborn. I was a young mother who was growing up with her kids. For most of their lives, I felt more like the sister than the mother.

**Day of Reckoning**

Spring 2001 was in full bloom, and I planned a Mother's Day trip with Ashley, who was seventeen at the time, and Jessica, fifteen. We loaded up the black Infinity for a girls' weekend in Tahoe. The trees were in full bloom showing off their vibrant green leaves as they danced in the gentle breeze.

Before we hit the road, I went into the house to the small little bathroom with its tiny window and the pale-yellow walls for a tune-up. I ignored the person I saw in the mirror and took out the little baggie of white powder. I dumped a pile of the powder on the countertop. I used the red and white straw and sniffed the white crystal powder into my left nostril.

Immediately I felt the heat rise into my skull, and the euphoric feeling took me away on a road trip of my mind. I got lost in my endless thoughts. Those first few hours of the high, I forgot all about those negative thoughts that told me what a horrible person I was. I forgot about all the detestable things I had done in my life. That poisonous powder gave me a false sense of happiness for a few hundred minutes, and that was all that mattered. As I reached for the doorknob, I caught a glimpse of myself in the mirror. I ignored the sadness in my eyes.

As I slid into the driver's seat, I felt the girls' mood had changed. Ashley, with her light brown hair falling onto her shoulders, was silent and stared straight ahead. I could sense that something was bothering her. As I looked into the rear-view mirror, I felt Jessica's eyes burning a hole in my back. Jessica has never been the type to hide how she feels. I felt the tension and the frustration as we drove down the gravel driveway in silence.

I knew they could tell I was using again, and the tension in my stomach created a heat that rose from my belly. I reached behind the seat for a beer.

Jessica broke the silence. Her voice, tense and stern, said, "When are you going to stop using drugs?"

At first, I didn't respond. I pretended not to hear Jessica. When I finally spoke, like a professional addict, I pushed the question back onto her. "What is your problem? What do you think you know about me?"

Jessica says, "I know you're using drugs again. I can tell."

"You can tell what?"

I was numb to what they were saying, and it had little effect on me. The numbing agent of meth was working. It was more painful for them than for me at that moment. The beautiful drive through the Sierras was fraught with begging and pleading.

"Mom, we know you're high. Why can't you admit it?"

"Admit what? The both of you don't have a clue."

"Mom, please stop using drugs."

I took another chug of my beer. The pressure was starting to get to me. But I stayed calm. By the time we made it to Tahoe, the two of them were crying and pleading with me to quit. My buzz started to wear off, and they were getting to me. I hit the bathroom and dumped a pile of the white powder out; my heart was pumping, adrenaline was flowing, anger was beginning to rise from deep inside of me. Just as I was sniffing the pile of meth, Jessica opened the bathroom door. Feeling numb, I returned from the bathroom, acting as if nothing had happened. Jessica was crying, and I insisted she stop her sniffling because she was ruining our weekend.

Ash and Jess have seen me abstain from drugs, and they have seen me in my darkest hours. The two of them have been watching after their mother their entire life. Making sure I was safe instead of me keeping them safe.

That day they were relentless in wanting me to quit, and I could feel the heat of anger rising from the depths of my belly. My armpits were sweating, my mouth was dry, and I began to scream and yell. I was about ready to crack. I couldn't keep up the insanity of my lies, which made me angry. Round and round, we went with me denying I had a problem. We rode home in silence. Jessica was in the back seat, Ashley in the front, both stifling their sad, angry tears. I was out of meth, so I drank my way home.

As we drove up to the big red barn to park the car, Rick stood there with his hands in his pocket. Shoulders rounded and defeated. My heart sank; I could feel something was off. Rick and I had lived together for the past year and a half. Rick was a big teddy bear of a man, the kind that makes you feel safe. From the day we met, he was the first person I felt was safe. I knew Rick loved me, and it would take me years to realize how much.

Upset and angry, the girls quickly grabbed their belongings and headed for the little cedar house. I slid out of the front seat and cautiously walked toward him.

My mind was scrambling to figure out what was going on. The buzz from the beer dissipated, and I can remember seeing the pain in his eyes. They were bloodshot as if he had been crying. My hands and feet felt cold, shaking from the inside out. I knew that something was about to happen. He began to weep when he looked at me. When he finally spoke, his voice cracked.

"Are you having an affair?"

Relief washed over me, and my body relaxed, and I began to think again. I was relieved because I had been defending my lies all weekend. This question I could answer somewhat honestly.

"No, I'm not having an affair with another man."

In retrospect, I was having an affair with drugs. Rick's next question was, "Who is John?"

My heart tightened, my throat restricted, and the guilt and shame coursed through my body. Soon that familiar voice from that day in the cabin spoke clearly from my heart: *Denise, you made a pact with yourself that if you ever felt the need to lie to another man you loved about your drug use that you would confess and quit for good.*

My eyes met Rick's, and we both began to cry.

"I'm not having an affair. I have a problem. I'm addicted to al-cohol and meth. John is my drug connection. I need help."

His large gentle hands took mine, his gaze never leaving mine.

When he finally spoke, his voice was shaky, and his tears of guilt and shame said, "I have a problem with alcohol, and I need to quit."

We stood in that big barn with its concrete floor, holding each other and crying for the relief of speaking the truth. I sank into Rick's arms, my shoulders releasing the tension of the lies. I let my guard down, and I felt safe, light, and relieved that I no longer had to keep up the lie. I finally had the courage and the strength to let go of my profound dark secret, and in turn, it helped this strong, caring man admit that he had a problem too. Sobbing and shaking, I could feel his strong arms holding me, which gave me the courage to do the next thing he asked of me. That was to go inside and tell my beautiful daughters that I had a problem with alcohol and drugs and needed help.

Sharing with my daughters that I needed their support to quit brought me relief, shame, and guilt. The relief I felt was about no longer having to lie about my secret. I felt responsible for the pain my addiction had caused them. The embarrassment and the shame of lying to them all weekend had me feeling guilty. I believe that my daughters had waited a long time to hear those words. Shocked and relieved, Jessica was the first to speak.

She asked Rick, "Are you going to ask my mother to leave now that you know the truth?"

"No. I will support your mother just like you will in any way to help her get off the drugs."

I don't recall Ashley saying much of anything. She just cried. I think they were both relieved the fight was over.

I had never asked for help before. Asking for help meant I was weak like my mother. I had finally given up the fight, and I didn't know how I would get sober. Before, I would abstain from drinking and drugging by exercising excessively. That would last for a few months until I got bored and overwhelmed with my life. I would go back to drinking and using drugs. I didn't even know how to ask for help because I never considered it a problem.

## Sobriety

The following day, I woke up to the sun shining and the bright blue sky overhead, and that inner voice calling me to go outside. As I stood facing the river with the pine trees next to me, I dropped to my knees and began to talk to God for the first time.

"God, all I want is to have a wise, trusting relationship with my-self. I want to know who I am. I want to be able to trust myself." Little did I know I had already begun to trust myself.

Each day after, that unmistakable voice guided me as she had always done. There was no way I could avoid her voice. Soon she would drive me to meditate. At first, I didn't even know what it meant to meditate, so I started sitting outside in my hot tub with my eyes closed. In the beginning, meditating was uncomfortable and foreign. I didn't understand what I was doing. That voice kept encouraging me to sit still. Rain or shine, I sat still daily.

Soon I found a rehab program. It was a county-funded program, mostly for people who had been court-ordered to attend. I happen to be one of the only volunteers. I didn't know how to get sober. I didn't even know that such programs existed.

A few days into the program, a male counselor asked me why I drank and used drugs. The words flew out of my mouth. "Why wouldn't I?" Drinking, drugging, lying, and cheating didn't seem abnormal.

As the weeks went on, we sat in the same circle of metal chairs, sharing our secrets. I noticed a common theme among them – they were all suffering from sexual abuse. I remember being relieved that that had never happened to me. The very next day, a woman shared her story about sexual abuse, and I felt a sensation deep in my belly. The energy from my stomach began to move up into my heart, and I heard myself gasp for air. At that moment, I knew that I was suffering from repressed sexual abuse. It was the voice of knowledge that spoke, and I knew it was true. It would take me another fifteen years to realize my addiction to alcohol and drugs covered the emptiness I felt inside from being abandoned by my mother and sexually abused by my father.

The pain from the shame and the guilt I felt would stay with me for two long years. The endless mind chatter about whether to drink or not to drink, to use or not to use, was the daily conversation in my mind. I battled with my inner voice, haunted by what a horrible person I thought I was. This created so much confusion. Life became one depressing moment after another. I knew there was no turning back, but I wanted to escape the reality of the pain.

After the rehab, I attended Alcoholics Anonymous (AA) for about five years and received support and understanding of my addiction. I returned to exercising, doing endless amounts of walking in the forest, meditating, and spending lots of time reading the Bible and searching for my understanding of God. My spiritual journey began the day I decided to become clean and sober. I have been sober and meditating for over twenty years.

Rick and I shared the secrets of addiction. Neither of us was able to admit that we had a problem until that day. In retrospect, that weekend was a battleground for the truth. Sometimes you meet the perfect mate for reasons that keep revealing themselves. I have never doubted my relationship with Rick. We have walked through many fires in our twenty-two years together. I grow and move forward on my awakening, and he never ceases to amaze me. He meets me with his internal knowledge. They say we come to this earth plane for one person. I know who my one person is.

I know today that I have broken the cycle of addiction in my family. My daughters know a different way of living. After being sober for a year, my mother got sober.

**"I can never get full. I'm not enough."**
My capacity to love is endless. Yet, I fear that I'm not enough of anything. My experience with my mother began as a lack of nurturance and abandonment. From what I have learned from working with therapists and energy healers, my mother was stressed during my infancy. Her

mother didn't raise her; her sister brought her up, so she was unable to, nor had a desire to meet my needs as a mother should.

One of my first male teachers, Chris, an intuitive psychologist, asked me, "Why did you choose your parents?" At the time, it was the craziest thing I had ever heard. But I knew at that moment that I had chosen my parents. I chose the perfect parents not to love and nurture me. Part of my experience in this lifetime has been to turn inward towards my inner being for love. If I had had the perfect mother, I wouldn't have kept searching for the connection to my innermost being.

By age five, my life became all about my mother's happiness. I felt everything my mother was going through. I wasn't able to just live like a little girl. I always felt *not enough.* As I grew older, I lived in a constant state of fear that something was wrong with me. My life felt empty, and I felt lost. I couldn't figure out where I belonged or how to belong. I was constantly referencing others to understand how I was to feel or act.

I gave away my power to my mother's well-being, all the while ignoring my sense of self. I often felt like a victim and later learned I took on my mother's feelings of victimhood. All I wanted was to be enough for my mother so she would be happy. If I could make her happy, it would be safe for me. I felt like I was always fighting for my happiness. I always ended up feeling like an abandoned, abused child.

I learned from reading Steven Kesslers's book *The 5 Personality Patterns*, Barbara Brennan's book *Light Emerging*, and Regina Stribling from the *Labyrinth of Illumination* healing that I gave my whole self to others. Joining my energy with others to relate to them would entangle me with their dramatic affairs. By merging my power with them, I felt what others were feeling. I took on their emotions, causing myself pain and suffering that wasn't my own. I didn't know that I shouldn't do this. Merging my energy with others cheats them out of their emotional experiences and leaves me confused about who I am. One of the most valuable lessons I have learned on this life journey is that, when you free yourself from the pain and guilt, you have caused another human being, you stop holding them hostage.

My healing comes from my willingness to see what I intuitively already know. To heal the fear of not being enough or lovable, I have to be still with myself and ride the emotions of my worries. I have to be willing to sit with what I know to be true. My worst fear is not getting enough love, which feels like abandonment. Each time I showed up to meditate, I went within and loved myself, creating a connection with my Soul, strengthening my ability to hear the voice of my Spirit.

# Chapter 6

# Spirit Speaks

*"Spirit is Life Loving Itself."*
~Anand Mehrotra

I remember the day Rick and I were riding our road bicycles down Schaad Road, and we came up with the name for my personal training business. Bouncing names off each other, we created *Bodies N Balance*.

*Bodies N Balance* was motivated by a statement that I heard in Alcoholics Anonymous: "As an alcoholic and addict, I was a selfish person who only took from society." That pissed me off and I vowed to myself to give back. I had already received my certification as a Personal Trainer and worked at a couple of the local gyms. I didn't like working out or working in gyms. *Bodies N Balance* began as a mobile, in-home, personal training service.

Next, I created a business model and trained clients in a private training studio. I gave each client my undivided attention for one hour at a time. In my eyes, I was now a productive member of society. I took that one statement and made it a career to give back. Unbeknownst to me, my selfishness would become selflessness. My co-dependency would become an insidious part of the business.

Over the next nine years, *Bodies N Balance* grew from a small, four hundred square foot, one-room studio to a three thousand square foot building housing eight trainers, three yoga instructors, and a nutritionist. I crafted a franchisable business model with the help of a businessman who had franchised fitness business models. The business was profitable and unique enough to open a second location nearby. I was able to sell investors on my idea and raised $250,000 to franchise *Bodies N Balance*.

One day, during a personal training session, my client shared an experience at a retreat in Big Sur. She met an Indian guru. Since we shared similar spiritual perspectives, I was interested to hear what she had to say. She said, "I think you need to meet this Indian guru. He guides people on motorcycles through India."

As an avid motorcycle rider, my interest peaked. She shared with me how he recently made a documentary about his motorcycle journey called *The Highest Pass*. That night, I went home, watched the film, and signed up to go on Anand's next motorcycle adventure, which was two months away. In the meantime, Rick and I went to Ojai to meet him for the first time. For ten years, I meditated daily, had begun a regular yoga practice, and I was ready to deepen my understanding of my connection with Spirit.

I remember the first time I met Anand. He was dressed in a creme-colored Kurta, sitting upon a cushioned rock under a big old oak tree, his tender eyes smiling as he greeted me. The closer I came to him, the more I felt as if he saw through me. At that moment, I felt ashamed of what he saw. I hid behind Rick's ample frame. Unaware at the time, I caught a glimpse of something I had never seen in another human being. I was awed, and I wanted to get a closer look, but I didn't want him to see me. I walked through the bushes to look closer without him noticing me again. What I saw was gentleness, grace, and kindness that felt comforting.

That night, Spirit came to me. *Dear Child, what you saw in him was yourself as the illumination of love. You couldn't handle seeing the truth of who you are, so you hid in the bushes. Symbolic of how you have been hiding from yourself. You saw your innocence as the Divine in another human being, and this knowing scared your big ego.*

For three days, Anand took us on yoga journeys where we chanted, did heart-opening kriyas, endless prana breathing practices with Hatha Yoga that brought us out of our heads and into our hearts. When he began to play the harmonium on the third day, the melody spoke to my heart. My body responded by shaking and releasing the protective armor of anger that I had wrapped around my heart. The sweetness of Anand's voice sang to my soul, and my heart cracked open enough for me to let my Spirit in and release my soul's anger.

Tears flowed as I began to grieve the loss of my childhood innocence. Memories flooded my heart of a time when I knew the power of love – weeping and sobbing, waves of emotions washed over my heart.

*Dear Child, I saw you all curled up in a ball, protecting your little girl's heart. You saw me through the cracked doorway of your opening heart. The longer Anand's sweet-sounding voice sang that beautiful song, and the more tears flowed of lost memories of a time when we were living freely from your heart. Finally, seeing what had always been there. A part of you was dying. The love you felt in your body was intense – the illusion of an ego-mind dying from a false identity of unworthiness. Your strong mind was stepping aside to allow for that moment of deep connection to me. Vulnerable and open, physically held in Rick's solid and loving arms, held in the arms of Anand's voice as you allowed yourself to be loved. You surrendered all your fake fears to be held by two Divine men.*

I still hadn't any understanding of what was happening. On that sunny summer day, I let all those strangers see me, in my truth, and nothing terrible happened. My brave soul allowed the emotional experience of love to loosen the noose I had tied around my heart, keeping me from feeling passion.

The essence of the abandoned, abused child kept me hidden from the truth. I became identified as my physical appearance, full of muscles that created a coat of armor to cover up unworthiness. At the time, I became trapped in the false identity of a successful business owner and a personal trainer attached to the external egoic world. The tightness in my body resulted from a perception I created in my mind that I was unlovable, stupid, and unworthy of love, leaving me feeling empty and isolated on the inside.

*Dear Child, you showed up for you and me on that day. Your courage helped you see that you had gone astray. Your willingness to know the truth is what broke you open that day; you allowed me to blow some life into you, spurring you to travel to India with Anand to go deeper in. Your innocence is so sweet; your will so strong to discover the truth of who you are – aware of my presence guiding you to explore the unknown.*

**Worthy of Love**

I had no idea what I was in for. I was willing to travel to India, a country I never wanted to visit. The adventure to India was to face all my fears. Fears of poverty, filth, and not being safe.

Rick, who was always up for an adventure, was curious and fascinated by my willingness to grow. It sparked him to explore his spirituality. The two of us committed to our destiny to co-create a lasting spiritual relationship built on deep love and evolution.

The lease deal on the second location for Bodies N Balance was falling apart. And I was tired of pushing on the franchise and the opening of the second location. I decided not to sign the lease and let the pieces fall where they may. Deep down, I knew part of me didn't want to franchise and own a second location. But up until then, my ego drove me to believe that I wanted more success, more money, and more acknowledgment that I was enough. I knew I was taking a journey to change my perception of myself and my life. I was ready for my life to change.

I was excited about the India trip. We landed in New Delhi two days before my forty-seventh birthday. The following day we took a six-hour-long taxi ride to Rishikesh. Along the way, I took in how people lived. The people's poverty made me sad, but the Indians just accepted what was. The scent of plastic garbage burning alongside the road nauseated me. Indian spices perfumed the air filling me with a sense of culture. Enormous statues to honor Shiva were the size of ten-story buildings.

I noticed Indians leaving the temples with red dots on their foreheads. Some temples looked like stalls with statues inside. Some had ornate round tops with gold paint. Cows and stray dogs roamed the dirt streets eating garbage that the Indians left wherever they felt. Motorcycles, cows pulling carts, large trucks hauling goods, and cars racing along in a way that looked chaotic but felt orchestrated. Every town was lined with little stalls of Indians selling food, trinkets, house goods. There was something in the air that I was unable to understand. It was as if an unseen presence was holding me. Off to Rishikesh, we went on a twenty-one-day motorcycle journey into the Himalayan Mountains to the Spitty Valley.

*Dear Child, do you remember that first night in Rishikesh sitting on that boulder next to the river edge, the full moon illuminating the night? You heard my voice calling you; shine your light and stop hiding from yourself. With tears flowing, you answered me with,* no more hiding. *Your raw emotions began to flow through your body as you let go of the fear. The fear of being seen as the love of the light started to disappear, and soon you allowed me in your body, levitating for a moment until you began to realize that you were floating on air. That night you finally understood that you had been avoiding your love. You decided to shine your light as the love. After that night, I began to work through Anand to show you who you are. The ability to hold a container of love for all humanity to live in Divine love. That's how powerful you are, my dear child. You are the love.*

Two days later, seventeen of us from all around the world began following the Indian guru down profoundly rutted dirt roads on Royal Enfield motorcycles. After we crossed the bridge in Rishikesh, the group got separated. As soon as I realized that I was the leader, I got scared and didn't know which way to go. Fear of making a wrong turn made it difficult to respond. Suddenly there was a big bend in the road, and I felt something pulling me to go left up a steep hill. The energy pulling me in that direction was so intense that I forgot to pull in the clutch, and I crashed into Anand's motorcycle. I stalled out the first day's ride waiting for his bike to be repaired on the side of the road by the mechanics traveling with us.

Anand laughed at me and asked in his joking way, "What happened?"

"I forgot to pull the clutch when I put the brakes on."

*Dear Child, you thought it was the sharp turn and riding on the opposite of the road that threw you off, but later, you could see how Anand got into your head. He has a way of teaching you lessons without words. FYI you stopped trusting me the moment you got on the bike. Back in your head, my dear, most of those thoughts are not even your own.*

The next lesson that appeared was for me to ride at the back of the pack. All perfectly planned by Spirit to test me once again on my ability to trust Spirit. The back of the group was not where I wanted to be. I felt ashamed as if I had done something wrong. My ego wasn't happy with being the last one. Soon old fears of abandonment crept into my strong mind – that ego always wanting to be seen upfront behind the guru.

No one could see me, and I felt like a fool. I knew I was a good rider, yet I made a stupid move. Each time a rider backed off the throttle, I would fall off the back again. Fear of being stranded forced me to grab the throttle to keep Rick in my sights. Fear of abandonment had me feeling like there was no end in sight.

*Dear Child, those continuous thoughts that are not even yours leave you unable to differentiate which ideas are yours – lost in a world of random thoughts, creating a life of boomeranging emotional experiences, showing you how you have been living from thinking in your head. Now, do you understand my frustration to blow your mind apart? You were bobbing in a sea of your thoughts. Not knowing who you were, just connecting to every random thought like it was your own. I watched you patiently, never judging, as you went back and forth from your head to your heart.*

Each time I landed in my heart, I would rejoice. Tears of appreciation flowed. Gratitude filled my gut and expanded in my heart. The feeling of love had me noticing that the mountains resembled my strength and courage.

The more comfortable I got riding in the back, the more settled I became about being alone. Steady each day as I chose to ride to the left. Trusting my gut, no matter what obstacle showed up. It took me a few days to get up to the middle of the pack. Soon everyone wanted to ride behind my back.

As the days went on, I settled into the group and found my groove. Centered and safe in my inner world connected to the present moment. I was unaware that I held the entire group in a container of love – the light of love shining through me.

*Love, my dear, is your gift – the ability to hold the container of love and never know how it changes others. Your Divine love changes the world. Your gift is the ability to love. Your gift is deep compassion for other people's pain. It has allowed you to find forgiveness and acceptance for other souls' journeys on this Earth plane. I have given you the gift of seeing others' lessons from the pain you can see in their bodies. You teach them how to feel the pain to escape their stories of a life of suffering that keeps them from receiving love. You have this ability not to judge other people's journeys and honor them for their choices and understand their Soul experiences. Your gift of Grace to shine the light on the darkness. You have the gift of illuminating the darkness to know the light.*

Smooth and steady is how I rode, giving all the boys a run for their lives. I began challenging Anand with my strength and discipline to stay focused as I rode behind him. Anand was unable to drop me. I focused on my Spirit as I raced up the Himalayan Mountains behind him, leaving the pack behind. Anand stopped and began laughing and shaking his head at my ability to ride and keep up with him. I used my mental focus to stay centered as I challenged him. He stopped doubting me that day as I questioned his masculinity. He honored my ability to stand toe to toe, balancing my masculine and feminine showed him my courage to go deep to grow.

My deep commitment to know myself cracked me open a little more on that trip to India. Anand mirrored the power of my light. My light is just as bright as anyone else's light. Before I left, Anand told me that I didn't need a guru. He said, "You have already been the guru and the spiritual master. Now you just need to remember all the wisdom that is within you." He gave me a personal mantra, a daily affirmation with the citrine mala (necklace). He instructed me to silently whisper this mantra one hundred and eight times with my daily meditations, without knowing the meaning of his statement or the personal mantra. I went home and devoted myself to this new addition to my daily practice, and boy was I in for a ride of self-discovery.

# Chapter 7

# So-Called Success

*"Success is self-satisfaction."*
~ Unknown

In the corner of the Safeway shopping center sat *Bodies N Balance*. A sign in big, bold, blue letters marked the front of the building. I can still remember the first time I saw that three-thousand-foot location. I was excited and full of passion for growing my business. My ego grew to match the size of the building, and I found myself wrapped up in making money and being perceived as successful. I would go on to become the go-to fitness guru in my community. I joined forces with local upscale members of the community to raise thousands of dollars for local charities. I lured my daughter Ashley to join me in the business with the intention that she would take over my legacy one day. The two of us were a remarkable team.

When I left for India, I left the operation of the business in my daughter's capable hands. Returning from India, I can recall that first day back to the studio. I was driving past the front door and noticed my name plastered in bright blue letters. I felt this sensation tingle up my spine, and I heard Spirit say, *Dear Child, look how far you've come! You are the proud owner of a successful business.* I usually ignored that complimentary voice. I felt the overwhelming emotions bubbling up from a childhood of not being enough. I wasn't able to acknowledge how far I had come.

That day I was driving my red Mercedes GLK 350 with its twenty-inch chrome wheels and reflecting on why I bought that car. The red Mercedes screamed, "Look at me! I am a successful business owner!" My ego wanted everyone in the community to know that I had overcome my poverty-stricken childhood and my addictions. I owned the car, the business, the house, the great children, the perfect marriage. I finally felt like I was somebody. But who?

I parked at the back of the building, unlocked the glass door, walked into my office, turned on the light, and looked around. Everything looked the same, yet it all felt strange. Soon the trainers began to arrive for their morning clients. Settling back into the daily routine, I felt indifferent about my business. I felt empty and disconnected from my life.

Something inside of me shifted during my trip to India. I no longer felt the passion for succeeding as a franchisee chain of *Bodies N Balance* studios. That dream felt like a lifetime ago. I decided to return the investment money to the investors. Each investor was stunned yet respectful of my decision. I felt happy and expanded in my heart center for honoring my truth, but I tried to return to my life before India.

**Identity Crisis**

I can't remember how much time passed before everything I knew and everyone around me began to fall apart. The feeling of bliss from the experiences in India started to fade. I doubted the creation of my life. Feelings of anger and sadness overwhelmed me most days. I became an emotional wreck. Unable to stay focused and serve my clients, I knew that something was shifting inside of me. I didn't know who I was anymore. I felt like a fraud, which created shame. I felt like a nobody, and confusion overwhelmed me. The more confused I became about who I thought I was, the crazier my thoughts became.

That little girl, a stupid nobody, began to control my days and haunt my nights. Self-doubt and fear overwhelmed me, and I didn't want anyone to know that I was dying inside. My life was falling apart, and I kept asking myself (my mind), *What is wrong with you? Why can't you pull yourself and this business together?* All my old tricks to motivate myself weren't working. I created a story that my life would improve if I got rid of the business, so it wasn't surprising that the company slowly began to deteriorate.

As a leader, I had lost my confidence in my ability to lead my team. I desperately tried to keep up the old image as a professional business owner/wife/mother/personal trainer. Soon the people around began to leave.

The first to go was Dominic. He had a lot of charisma and brought a lot of positive energy to the studio. I adored him like I would my son if I had one. What was so interesting about this relationship was I felt he was the son I had aborted at age sixteen. Because I played the role of the mother in this relationship, I created the dysfunction. I became addicted to being the one to make others' lives better.

Unaware of what was happening, there was a familiarity with the sensations of betrayal and abandonment when he said he was leaving. Rage filled my thoughts, and I knew Dominic was not telling me the whole truth. My body reacted, and heat began to rise from my belly. The energy of anger moved up into my chest, where my heart contracted, and then up into my head. Something was off. Soon I found out that he was opening his own business in my old location.

When my daughter Ashley found out that she was pregnant with her second child, she told me she would be leaving once the baby was born. And I gave up on the business a little bit more. Ashley's energy is beautiful, joyful. She has a powerful energy, and she brings happiness wherever she presents her power. She was an asset to my business, and we had an arrangement that the company would be hers one day… until my granddaughter, Mackenzie, was born.

I can see today how my over-giving in business created dysfunction in my relationships with my team. I felt like I was in control when I over-gave. I thought I would make things easy for people to be successful. I encouraged them and supported them in whatever way I could. If they wanted more clients, I got them more clients. If they needed more training, I paid for it. I always believed that this was how you conducted business. All the while, I was manipulating them to stay. I over-gave so people wouldn't leave me.

I was unable to separate my business relationship from my friendships. My idea of being in a relationship was to make sure that their life got better, like I was God or something. Now I can see how this makes people feel trapped. I have so much love to give, yet I didn't have boundaries for expressing that love. My gift and curse are my ability to see the best in everyone. I can accept these relationships as my teachings. Without those experiences, I would never have seen how I controlled people with my over-giving. I gave my power to others in my relationship, and it always left me feeling abandoned and misunderstood.

When I changed the plan not to franchise and expand the business, there was no motivation for the others to stay. Before leaving for India, I decided that Dominic was not qualified to manage the second location. My over-giving with Ashley ran its course, and she was tired of feeling indebted to me for the money I lent to her five years prior. The decision not to expand and franchise showed a lack of motivation to be in business entirely. I wanted to quit, and I felt like a failure.

I kept pushing myself to fit into my perception of what society said I should be. I lived by a set of societal beliefs (that I made up) that said I should drive an expensive car, be successful in business, live in an upscale neighborhood, and have a perfect family. I had built a house of cards on these beliefs. My ego-mind had identified itself with this external world. And I believed that I needed all those things to fit into this world. No wonder I found myself reeling from the crumbling of this little empire that I thought was me.

The fear of not fulfilling my five-year lease and having to pay all that money to get out of a legal contract kept me fighting for another year. Staying in fear sent me into another downward spiral that had me fighting for survival.

The studio steadily continued to decline. The stress of losing money and keeping up this false identity was getting to me, and soon I couldn't think straight, and I could not make the simplest decisions. The quality of my work was declining because I was unable to function. The shame I felt about taking people's money for a service I provided that was less than optimal. I knew my heart wasn't in it. I was going home and waking up each morning asking the Universe for a sign to close the business. I can remember asking each day: *Is it time to complete the company?* And I would get the same answer: *Be patient and wait.* I got to know that voice well. I would beg and plead to make each new day the day to quit.

I'm not saying this was easy. I struggled with letting go, yet each time someone left, I began to lose a little more of myself, which meant that I was losing the identity I spent my life building.

## Health Crisis and Letting Go

I hated who I'd become. I was lazy, and I didn't care about anything anymore. When I didn't even have the energy to get out of bed, I knew something was physically wrong with me. I went to my holistic nutritionist and found out that I was malnourished. My body was unable to absorb the nutrients from the healthy diet I ate. I had a leaky gut and a nervous system that was working overtime.

I remember at that moment the unbelievable sadness I felt. I spent my whole life caring for my body, and it pained me to know that I had hurt myself. My heart broke at that moment, and I felt abandoned once again.

I had harmed my body by not expressing my emotions or handling my feelings. I was still trying to contain those traumatic experiences from my childhood. I was trying to be someone that I wasn't. I had been hiding my true inner self. The nervous system controlled my fight or flight system, and I worked overtime to keep my ego safe.

I could no longer keep this charade up. I needed to let go, and I believed the business and my earthly life needed to change. But I didn't know how to change.

All I knew was that I was a failure. The sadness I felt for the harm I had done to myself left me depressed. I ignored the overwhelming regret that pulled on my heart. Depression didn't exist in my world, yet I was despondent, trapped, lost, and alone. Once again, I felt like an outcast in the world, not being understood, my spiritual self not being understood, and most of all, I didn't understand what was happening to me.

One day, I felt a wave of knowing wash over me, and I knew that I had finally decided. I was closing the business, and I didn't care about the money, or other people's thoughts, or that the lease was due. The sense of relief washed over me because I'd finally admitted to myself this charade of a life was over.

I went home and prayed to God, and I asked when I should let this business go. No answer came at that moment, so interesting that I always believed those answers came immediately. Most of the time, the voice inside answered in mysterious ways.

Two days later, during my meditation, that voice said, *"Time to go."* I knew what that meant. It just so happened that day I had a meeting with my attorney. He told me how much it would cost to get out of the lease and suggested I find someone to sublease the building. I immediately got on the phone and began to call realtors, asking them if they knew anyone that wanted to lease my space. By the second call, I had a tenant. I remember asking the realtor when they would like to move in, and she said tomorrow. She asked me when I wanted to leave, and I said tomorrow. Ten days later, I dismantled my business and closed *Bodies N Balance* once and for all.

I had waited and sat still every day for two years, waiting for the Universe to align. This experience taught me to listen and be patient while the shitstorms were swirling around me. India taught me how to hear the voice of Spirit. I had battled with listening to my voice my whole life. All the while, I was consulting with my spirit voice for the proper answer when the going got tough.

I can see now that the trap is my ego-mind. I thought I was my thoughts. Believing my thoughts kept me trapped in a material world that left me feeling that suffering was the only way. I fell for the ego-mind trap until I became aware of my thoughts. Today, I catch myself thinking those less-than-good thoughts, which are not my truth. All I know now is that my ego-mind is strong, and I have a strong will that, at times, won't let me give up.

Today I can see when I'm being pulled outside my center by my ego's desires for comfort and money. When my ego-mind is in control, I want material things, and I cannot accept or be with what is. I'm unable to be with the pain of my feelings and emotions. When I come to my center, I can accept what is because my yoga teacher taught me the Universe is always working for me. My ego-mind is all about the external human experience, the tangible things that we believe provide comfort and love.

## Spirit Speaks Again

*Dear Child, back home to a made-up reality, constructed from all those thoughts of an identity that matched an external world that you thought you should be. A business owner, personal trainer,*

91

*yogi, wife, grandmother, and the authority left you feeling trapped. Trapped in an identity that no longer fits the person you saw while riding in India, trapped in a story constructed from the thoughts that you weren't enough.*

*You saw that this life was no longer you but could not see your way out. Back to your mind, you lost contact with me once again. Being in your head created more abandonment; you could not understand why. You kept on pushing with all those great thoughts.*

*Meanwhile, I kept knocking and nagging at your heart. You asked me for help as you entered your heart. You did learn a lot about yourself in India, and you knew this life was not what you wanted. I had you wait for the right moment. All the while, you were practicing those Indian teachings to cultivate that love in your heart. There were those days you would beg me to end this tragedy. I would send you a sign of the hawk flying.*

*You would calm for a minute and go back to praying, misunderstanding the signals I sent. I watched you visualize between me and your ego-mind. You were trusting your mind to the point you would fall back into the trappings. Off into the world of your mind, "I'm a terrible person," "I'm so stupid," "I'm so lonely, nobody understands me." "I'm afraid to fail," "I'm such a fool." You forgot that I had just sent you a sign. It took me two years to get you to pay attention and realize that what you were longing for was right there inside you.*

*Not wanting to be different, you tried to keep the business going, yet kept on experiencing abandonment. I saw you crying and losing your mind. Your ego was dying. The old way of creating and fixing with your mind was no longer working.*

*The day finally came, and you heard me calling. Girl, you closed that business in less than two weeks, and off you went back to India.*

I learned that my spirit spoke to me in a gentler, kinder dialogue. My spirit is the inner Universe that supports me as I process my feelings and emotions while loving me from my goodness. I face my ego's fears head-on. My spirit resides in my core and speaks from a place of joy, love, and abundance. My soul is led by my heart and enjoys the human experience with all of its drama. I can finally hear the truth, even though sometimes the truth is hard to hear. I am good. I am loved and connected to my inner world, not the outer world's false materialism.

To completely understand and shift my life, I knew I needed to be in a highly conscious community that would support me in going deeper to discover my inner truth.

# Chapter 8

# My Healing Journey: A Return to Love

*"True Love is the self experiencing itself back again."*
~Anand Mehrotra

On November 8, 2017, I closed the business and leased out my home. Rick and I returned to the family ranch in the mountains to live in a thirty-seven-foot travel trailer while we figured out what to do next. I felt raw and cracked open and unable to comprehend what occurred in my life. The ranch, surrounded by trees and water, was a refuge for both of us during our transition. The solitude of nature comforted both of us.

I found out that Anand was offering a self-discovery retreat in January called The Warrior of Wisdom. I knew I needed to attend the retreat to help me transition into this new version of myself. For the first time in my life, I would go on an adventure alone. My one-month retreat would turn into a six-month-long experience of traveling to Egypt and living at the Sattva Center to attend a 300-hour yoga teacher training in Rishikesh, India, with Anand.

When I arrived at the Sattva Center, Anand greeted me with open arms. Soon I settled into a daily routine of morning Puja (a ceremony of offerings and honoring the Divine feminine), meditation, and yoga journeys. I spent my afternoons alone, roaming the hills of Rishikesh, having conversations with Spirit that had me begging to know my true identity.

My first lesson came when I noticed that Anand was ignoring me. Intuitively I didn't care; I wanted to be left alone. I came to Sattva to be with myself. I spent the time in the mountains, going inward and nurturing my heart. My connection to Spirit became easier to sense, and soon my thoughts were no longer occupying my head. Feelings of childlike innocence filled the center of my chest. I began to enjoy my alone time with Spirit. One day after returning from a walk, I came around a hedge, and Anand was holding out his arms with his joyful smile. When I entered his warm embrace, I knew he was happy to see me connected to my heart again.

The next time Spirit spoke was during a yoga journey where we had done endless naval pumping. Spirit appeared in my heart as Jesus cuddled me as an infant. Overwhelmed with the grace at Jesus's presence, tears of joy sprang from me, and I could hear Spirit say, *Dear child, I wanted you to see and remember that you have been a man like Jesus, and I honor thee. I wanted you to know you are benevolent in your journey, and your ability to walk this planet with such grace and honesty is as majestic as the Masters. Your love for me has always been a part of your destiny. I wanted to show you who you are in all of your glory, a female human of Jesus who loves humanity.*

The next time Spirit came to me, it was during the opening ceremonies. Mary Magdalene appeared right before me, showing me my femininity – compassionate, kind, and loving. Mary smiled and bowed to me. Flying high and feeling the love, I went on to hold the container of love for sixty people on the next day's yoga journey. Unaware of the intensity and the capacity of my love, I remember the woman that was standing next to me fainted. Spirit came to me later when I walked into the mountains. *Your lesson, my child, is your ability to find compassion for those who have harmed you. You bring the light of love to the earth plane for humanity. You are the life force that brings life to the planet. Just like Jesus and Mary, except you are both of them.*

The next lesson came during yoga teacher training. Anand showed up one day and taught a single Kriya, the Ram Kriya. I'm sure this Kriya was just for me. Because once the lesson was complete, I was in a trance and unable to move my body, and I remember hearing Spirit speak. *Denise, you must get back to your room.* Slowly, I walked to my room, and the moment I laid down on the bed, my body began re-enacting every man who had sexually abused me – my father, grandfathers, uncles, strangers. My body shook, contorted, and thrashed about, releasing the energies of traumatic sexual experiences in my childhood as I screamed and cried into a pillow.

I kept my mind focused on the pain my body expressed and ignored the victim stories that my mind threw up to distract me. I concentrated on my spirit and willed myself the courage to ride the wave of the energy that was leaving my body. Relieved, amazed, and reeling from all that I had seen, I sat in silence, and Spirit said *I love you, dear child, and thank you for following me.* My fear of knowing the truth of being sexually abused finally came out of me.

**Life on the Ranch**

Three months passed after returning home from my second trip to India. Still in the earlier stages of my second awakening, Rick and I decided to sell our home in the affluent neighborhood. We lived on the ranch, trying to develop a way for the land to support us without returning to regular jobs. I still wasn't ready and didn't know if I would ever be prepared to go back out into the world and work. Then we discovered that the county we reside in legalized marijuana farms. It seemed like a good way for us to earn some money until the house sold.

My main job was to water the female plants. Each day I entered the garden to water, the female plants greeted me with vibrant green buds with fuzzy white hairs. My nostrils filled with the sweet, musty, distinct smell of the female plants, sending tingles up my spine. Their budded branches reached up and out, calling for the male as she opened her flowers, waiting to receive his pollination. They danced freely in the wind and sent out their own unique, sensual, sexual scent.

Spirit spoke to me through those female plants and showed me how sensual, sexual energy flows. Those female plants expressed their sexuality without inhibition. Each unique female spoke to me with the power that she vibrated, igniting and heightening my psychic abilities. They communicated with my feminine desires to be expanded and loved, opening my heart just a little more. Those plants loved me, and I learned to nurture myself by unconditionally caring for them.

Soon the bliss bubble faded, and I began to use the strength of my mind to will myself to stay in that feeling of love. Focusing my mind on my heart created the feeling that I believed was love. Life became all about feeling the love. But I was willing this sense of love with my mind instead of allowing it to flow through me.

The stillness and the happiness bored my ego-mind, so it began to use the marijuana garden to make me believe that I was doing something wrong. *You're an addict just like your parents. What do you think you're doing? Only losers grow marijuana. Who the hell do you think you are? Remember, you came from drug-addicted parents who abused you sexually, emotionally, mentally, and used your energy for their desires. You know they never did care about you or your needs. They beat you and left you to raise yourself.* Gradually I began to slip back into my trauma drama.

My mind told me that I needed more fixing. *Maybe that last dive wasn't deep enough. Or perhaps you didn't fully understand the lesson from your childhood. I'm sure you'll find something else to heal if you keep looking.* My ego-mind loved to dredge up the past trauma as long as I was willing to dive into that history. And I was. I shoved my feelings of self-love down. Dove back into the depths of my pain and suffering to find one more piece of the abandoned, abused child to dissect, only to learn once again all of life was perfectly planned by me to see me.

# My Healing Journey

## Soul Contracts

For a year, I worked with Joseph, my master teacher friend, on soul contracts. He helped me to cut cords from soul agreements I made with my parents. But my ego continued to pull me into the emotions of the pain and suffering of sexual abuse, and most of all, my insecurities of not being enough. I became lost in my mind and convinced myself that something was wrong with me.

The main lesson was how connected I was to my mother's energy. I needed to separate from her to find myself. Soon, I saw how I over-loved my mother as a way to feel loved. It took me a long time to know that I AM the mother I desired.

While I worked with Joseph on soul contracts, I didn't get very far with my dad. My mother became the focus of my hatred, shame, and guilt. My soul contract with my mother was for her to abandon and abuse me as a way for me to learn how to love myself, along with ending the thousands of years of suffering and suppression of the women in my lineage.

I could handle hating my mother. But to feel anything about my father was not even in my consciousness at the time. It was almost like I didn't have a father; he didn't exist even though he was already dead by then. If I stayed focused on my mother, I would not (and could not) look at the relationship with my father.

Each time I completed my journey with another healer, I found myself high and in my love bubble, living in my heart space once again, and this was no different. Each time I recognized my soul contract with my mother, I moved to this new level of myself. I found myself waking up each morning in gratitude. I can remember recognizing that I loved my life. I had all I needed. Life was good. I could allow myself to be happy.

As soon as my life became calm and straightforward, my ego always led me to want more. It looped back into the obsessive thoughts that I wasn't enough. This time it was about money. I convinced myself that I had money issues that I needed to heal. My mind began its usual chatter, *"Something's wrong; you need help. Find someone to help you with these money problems, so you can once again be happy."*

## The Energy of Ancient Suffering

The soft gray truck seat pressed on the back of my thighs. My phone sat on top of the dash to get the strongest signal. I fiddled with the phone a little more and took a deep breath while I scanned the environment. My mind wandered to what was about to occur as I awaited the call of yet another healer.

The woman who had introduced me to Anand also led me to Kimberly. Kimberly was known for her energy clearings and her Wealth Without Worry program claimed to heal your money problems. Since returning from India, I hadn't been working. I was beginning to feel restless and concerned about money. Money became my new problem that needed healing.

I stared out the dust-covered windshield at the red dirt road and snapped back into reality when the phone rang, excited and sure that healing my issues around money would fix me once and for all. Still unaware, my mind was creating issues that there was something wrong with me. I embarked on another deep dive into the past.

I remember Kimberly instructing me to ground into the Earth. I began to feel this pulling sensation in my lower body. My firm, focused mind ignited my imagination and showed me the core of the Earth. Next, Kimberly instructed me to connect to the pure source of Christed energy through my crown. Once connected to the Earth's and the Christed power, she and I began to clear my chakras and aura. Kimberly taught me that my auric energy field held the trauma drama.

We were making our way into the second chakra of emotional stories when blood-curdling screams erupted out of me. My senses began to feel the pain of my mother. The emotions and feelings ran through my body, and my body started to contract, contort, shake, and spasm.

Kimberly's voice guided me to remove my mother's, grandmother's, and great-grandmother's old pain and suffering. Banshee screams continued to vibrate my throat chakra. Salty tears and snot ran down my face. Physically, I felt my belly releasing the emotional ancient dark pain of suffering. My mind and body, exhausted, finally let go of those long-lost stories that no longer served me or my lineage. The long line of feminine suppression left me weak, thirsty, and sad.

Joseph used to tell me those emotional stories weren't mine. Up until now, I never understood what he meant. Suffering was familiar and, in a perverse way, comfortable. I felt like I was doing something when I was suffering. And I believed the spiritual journey of healing needed to be painful to be helpful. Feeling the emotions of the trauma is unbearable. But I had made it my life's mission to keep feeling the pain of suffering. My mind was making me suffer, and my lack of knowledge on how the mind operates kept me in my prison. It took me a long time to see that I kept looping back into my mind. My lack and suffering were ancient, and these feelings kept me from trusting my relationship with Spirit and money. I learned that my relationship with not trusting money came from my father selling me to the child prostitution ring to settle his gambling debt.

I studied with Kimberly for about a year and learned how to use her energy healing technique to work with others. With the strength of my mind, my ability to read the emotional body, my connection to the Christed energy, I began to clear my energy field daily. I soon began to have a clearer image of my energy field. Kimberly validated that my gifts of seeing the emotional energies that were not flowing in other peoples' bodies were accurate. Recognizing my talent gave me the confidence that I needed to take the next step in my ability to heal others.

**Spiritual Bootcamp**

My mind started telling me that *I needed to get a job and make money, or I was going to run out of money and be stuck living in that ugly travel trailer forever.*

I had spent a lot of money over the past couple of years healing. I wanted to monetize this newfound healing gift that I discovered with my new knowledge of energy clearing, my certification as a life coach, my yoga certification, Reiki certification, and meditation certification.

One day, scrolling Facebook, I saw an ad for a Bootcamp for Spiritual Leaders. They were making promises that you could create an online healing business using Facebook and your healing gifts. The

Bootcamp sounded like the answer to my prayers. I could use my gifts to heal people from the comfort of my own home. Something didn't feel right about their promises, and I ignored my innermost being and paid the 10K.

Once again, I found myself listening to someone else instead of my innermost being. The leader of the Bootcamp convinced me I needed more healing before I could go out in the world and help people. I let my ego convince me that I was broken and needed fixing, and these people preyed on the thoughts that I was having about myself.

Joy and happiness left me once again. I'd gotten pulled back into my mind for some more healing. I noticed that no one in the group was moving forward. We were all stuck in our trauma, and there wasn't anyone there to guide us through the shit. That program left me more broken than I had felt in a long time.

**Illumination**

Feeling broken and needing someone to help me unravel what I had just experienced led me to a beautiful woman named Regina Stribling, who showed me the Divine Feminine's true meaning. She took me on a journey through the Labyrinth of Illumination, where I met my Spirit, the Goddess of Infinite Light.

The Labyrinth of Illumination helped me understand the effects of the trauma I experienced. None of the healers I had worked with taught me how I operated as a human who had experienced severe trauma. I was introduced to my anger defense and saw how I used anger to cover my sadness and fear.

When I experience anger, I know it comes from not being willing to look at why I feel sad. Anger is my cover-up for disconnection from my heart. It's my soul's way of letting me know that I'm back in my mind, operating from fear.

Regina loved me, and I responded to her love. She opened my heart a little bit more once again. I found myself back in my heart, full of that happiness that I promised myself to receive. I soon stepped into the online world with the first healing program that she helped me create.

During our time together, Regina opened my subconscious to the wound around my dad and my lineage. We took a journey into the depth of my belly, where the ancientness of my lineage was stored. There I saw my father's ancestors walking toward me from a dark tunnel. I remember I told her that they were all chained together at the neck, at the arms, and at the ankles. They were blank – like grey ghosts without souls, meaning they were soulless.

Today I see this as a metaphor of what happens when we live only from the ego-mind. Our soul becomes trapped in the matrix of the mind. To be trapped in this way is to lose sight of the light of your true nature. It occurred to me that my father had been imprisoned by his mind, leaving him soulless. Even before I began this work, I said that my father was a lost soul, but did not ever really understand what I was saying.

Regina helped me create my first healing program, *Heal Your Emotions, Release the Weight*. I helped others using my intuitive ability to see the emotions that were not flowing through their bodies. When the energy was released, it resulted in physical weight loss. The feeling I experienced with moving the emotional energy energized and uplifted me each time I guided others to release the emotional stories that kept them stuck. I had finally discovered how to use this knowledge of my spirit. I can remember in those early days being able to understand when my mind controlled the healings instead of my spirit, the Goddess of Infinite Light.

With each healer, I was able to reach another level of my remembering. As Anand had said, "You just need to remember all that you have already been." As I worked with each of these amazing healers, I balanced the negative and positive, masculine and feminine, dark and light within. To become neutral within myself enabled me to see all those aspects that hid around my periphery. I discovered that I am continuously evolving, becoming aware of when I need help.

I always had the expectation that I would somehow be "finished" with my healing journey. And, with more and more layers, deeper dives, I unlocked the next big phase of transformation in my life, what felt like a death of my ego, but more realistically was an integration of my soul. When we embrace life as a transformation toward remembering who we are, next thing we know we're two feet deep into the shit of it all.

# Part 3

# Ego Integration and

# Navigating Two Worlds

# Chapter 9

# Prisoner of The Mind

*"Mastering the Mind to Navigate the Heart."*
~Anand Mehrotra

I can see now that my journey has been one of awakening to my true sense of myself. My journey has been one of many battles: feeling safe in my body, understanding what my emotional stories were revealing to me, fighting for my soul to be connected to my spirit. Bringing all these parts of me in alignment has led to a synchronicity that has set spirit free to be expressed through me. At times, my journey has been excruciatingly painful and other times boring. Each phase has provided me with the lessons I needed to bring me one step closer to my truth.

The energy healing process with my clients also helped me. I started experiencing more and more spontaneous self-healing from all the energy clearing that I was doing. The truth was I still didn't understand that I was merging my energy with the sorrow of my clients. By believing that their pain was my own, I created those familiar feelings that something was wrong with me.

One day, after a difficult session with a client, I decided to go for a walk in the forest of our family's ranch to my favorite swimming hole called Slippery Rock. On that hot summer day, I remember the warmth of the rocks supporting my back while the sound of the rushing river drowned out my thoughts. My body relaxed. I closed my eyes and focused on my third eye, drawn into my navel center, where my spirit resides. The warmth of the sun made me tired, and soon I found myself dozing off as waves of emotional memories arose from the depth of my being. My spirit took me into another spontaneous healing as my mind flashed images of past sexual experiences.

Rumbling energy shot up throughout my entire body. The heat of anger was intense. I screamed and cried out to spirit for help. I can remember not being able to stand the pain that shook and contorted my body. Resistance in my body triggered my mind to return to the trauma of past emotional stories. I focused my strong mind on my core and brought my attention back to the wave of intense anger expressed by my body. I screamed, and then I roared like a lioness who was protecting her cubs. I clenched my teeth and made my hands into claws, and used my animal strength to yell through the pain of all those times I was unable to stand up for myself.

I watched the internal battle between my mind, body, and spirit. Soon the wave of emotional energy passed. I stood, mindfully stepped to the river's edge, plunged my naked body into the ice-cold water, and swam to cleanse myself of one more memory of the abandoned, abused child.

I felt more spacious and open as I dried my skin and slipped on my shoes, and walked the short steep climb through the forest home. I felt the spirit of the trees talking to me. The smell of pine warmed my senses. The needles crumbled underneath my feet. I crested the top of the hill and entered into the dense grove of maple trees growing along the edge of the Boston Gulch. There stood a wise old cedar tree. Her spirit called to me. I snuggled my back into her big belly.

As I tuned my energy into her, she began to whisper, *you can choose at this moment to stop telling that story of the abandoned, abused child.* I wept when I heard her voice. I felt the resistance of hanging on to the identity of the abandoned, abused child slipping away. I listened to my spirit speak through that wise cedar tree. I cried because I finally knew that the old story of the abandoned, abused child no longer served me. I chose at that moment to be loved by that wise cedar tree.

It never occurred to me that I had a choice to drop that old emotional story. The abandoned abused child's perception of love equated pain with love. I remember shaking my head in disbelief. How could I not see that I had a choice to feel love kindly?

As the summer went on, my mind would wander to that place, and I would simply remind myself that I had already chosen not to believe that old story. Most of that summer, I walked the forest, allowing the trees to remind me that spirit was in everything. Spirit spoke lovingly, kindly through the trees. I started seeing every living organism in nature as a spiritual experience. Walking in the forest expanded my heart, and I was reminded of being loved and connected to all that I saw: the steadiness of the trees, the green swaying grass, the sweetness of the flowers, the blueness of the sky, and the puffiness of the clouds.

That day under the cedar tree, I chose to become aware that it was my mind that was playing that familiar movie. My relationship with the trees brought me closer to the spirit of my soul in my body. I began to love all that I could see. Feelings and sensations ignited my heart each time I entered the world of the trees. My connection to nature expanded that summer. I began to rejoice and look up at the trees when I needed to feel the love of my spirit. With the trees, I felt safe just to be. For the first time in my life, it felt safe to be present and loving.

## The Final Death of the Old Me

Once again, I found my mind rambling over that the old story of the abandoned, abused child. I fought the rambling. Not able to stand the chatter, I called my teacher Maia, and she said to me, "Your ego is dying." Fear ran through me, and my mind and my jaw began chattering. I was finally grasping that it was all in my mind. The story of the abandoned, abused child was a groove in my brain that was so deep it kept pulling me back into an old identity. Until that day, my mind had not stopped identifying itself as the story, and my ego wanted the identity of the abandoned, abused child back.

Finally, the truth that I wasn't the abandoned, abused child sank in. My mind freaked by sending waves of fear to every cell in my body. Tension in my stomach, toes curled, knees locked, fist clenched, shoulders tight, neck stiff – my body responded to the lack of acceptance of my mind and the unwillingness to let go of the abandoned, abused child. My mind and body fought each other, unwilling to accept that the heart was now becoming the master.

Grief constricted my heart and prevented my mind from thinking incessantly. I began to understand that I wasn't my mind, but I still did not understand my spirit either. My body was confused and fought the sensation of love; my mind froze in fear. Chaos tore through my body, fear sprinted through my mind, the heart was on high alert.

I soon found myself in the middle of my living room, pulling at my hair, crying, and screaming into the phone as I yelled to Maia. Was I losing my mind? Was I going insane? Or was my mind losing control of my life? Not understanding what was happening, I felt confused and afraid. The ego-mind tried to hold on as I moved down into my core, connecting to my innermost being.

I remember Maia making me look at the image in my mind of myself sitting behind bars in my mind prison. I recognized that I was a little girl who was trapped in a concrete jail cell in the center of my head, huddled up in the corner, paralyzed by fear. I couldn't move the little girl I saw in my mind.

I heard Maia's voice on the other end of the phone encouraging me to stand up.

I screamed, "I can't stand up. I'm stuck."

I remember focusing with my mind and willing that little girl to stand up. She felt so heavy.

Finally, Maia said, "I'm here to help you stand up."

Focusing my mind on my six-year-old self's image in that prison cell, I began to will her to stand up. It was hard to get her to move. She felt cemented, and then suddenly, little by little, she began to rise. With the help of Maia's voice on the phone, we helped her stand up.

Stiff as a board, I saw myself standing up in my head, and my little girl stepped out of the prison of my mind. She stepped out of the darkness and into the light. I recognized that all of it was me. I was the only one keeping her trapped in the prison of my mind. In a daze of disbelief, I couldn't believe it was me all that time. I was imprisoning me. I finally chose to be free. I was laughing, crying, dancing, and screaming joyfully.

**Final Relief**

On my fifty-fourth birthday, I decided to go on a psilocybin retreat with Maia. Not knowing what to expect, and scared of what might happen, I trusted her and the process and went anyway.

On the first day, we journeyed to the beach. The mushroom began to have an effect, and my mind was vital as it fought the impact. It was pushing me to see my reality – the truth of what I already had been seeing. Spirit was in every living thing. Plants dancing in the wind vibrating at a frequency that I had seen in the forest.

I saw my resistance to letting go and being a part of nature. I was drawn to the light of the sun, knowing that I was the light. Distracted by the sand and irritated that I could not accept that I was dirty, I hated the sand and fought the reality that was grinding on me.

Finally, I began to laugh at my quirks, having to have everything perfect for me to be me. Surrender to the grit of the sand. I began to make swirling motions with my hands in the sand, circling and circling my hands until I let go and allowed myself to expand. Accepting the energy that I felt was me. I asked how to be in the world with all this energy. How do I accept myself as love?

I walked along the water's edge, relaxing into the realness of who I am. I am the love. I began to move my body as the Goddess of Infinite Light (Spirit), mixing the energy and bowing to the Divine within and laying my back on the rocky edge. I stopped complaining about who I am. Acceptance occurred that day on the beach. The acceptance of love and compassion made my heart hurt. I loved myself so much that day. I could never return to the old tune that I had played.

The pain of the past no longer held me. Kindness and joy filled my heart. I rested at last, free of all the hurts. Loving the light, I played by remembering who I have always been. A child loved by her mother was laying dormant within her belly, waiting for recognition. I loved the essence of my spirit. Warm, happy, and fun-filled heart. I played that day with nature in me. I honored my journey and became the real me. The light of my true nature is and always has been love.

On the next day's journey, I saw that I also liked playing in my sexual energy. The Divine love of my power feels so yummy to me. I also noticed that my sexual experience meant knowing that I was playing with my sensuality. Sexual abuse that happened to me should not be dismissed as an attack. It means that I wanted to experience my sexual reality. Forgiveness of myself for all my misery allowed me to let go of another layer of suffering.

On my way home, Maia encouraged me to stop and visit my mother. It was time for me to see her while dancing in my truth. It was finally time to see it all for its truth.


**Mom's Death**

I went to visit her on my fifty-fourth birthday. Mom was now in assisted living. She had been diagnosed with dementia three years prior, at age seventy, and could no longer care for herself. Over time she had started not to be able to recognize me. I would ask her, "Do you know who I am?" She would answer by saying, "You look like me." But she couldn't identify who that me was.

The home was located in a residential neighborhood where she had her own room off the big backyard. I had called ahead to let the home know that I was coming. When I arrived, she was sitting in the backyard under a big willow tree. I showed up with my heart open and a box of maple leaf-shaped cookies. Mom loved her sweet treats.

It didn't surprise me when I was invisible to her. I remember, during that visit, when she turned her eyes sideways, she got a glimpse of me. I knew she wanted to look at me, but I blinded her in all my glory. Rick, my mom, and I sat under that big old willow tree, shading ourselves from the late September heat as we ate the whole box of maple cookies. Rick played songs on his accordion that invoked memories of the good old times the three of us had spent working in the bar and putting on music events. The three of us sang together about living on the river, an old Credence Clearwater Revival song that made her smile about the fun times we had living on the ranch.

I finally felt safe being in her presence as the light of my true nature. Love. Our spirits were working things out, and I had this knowing that this would be the last time I would ever physically see her again. Our spirits let us both know that I had finally completed our soul agreement. Radiating, I turned to her in the lawn chair and silently thanked her for all my gifts.

My inner voice spoke. *Your soul Journey with her is complete.*

My human self was astonished at knowing that my soul was now whole. The abandoned, abused child ultimately integrated that day sitting next to my mother under the willow tree.

My inner being rejoiced and absorbed the knowledge that I had made it to the light. I knew she was proud of me. I had kept my word to find my way to the light of my true nature. I had kept my promise to find my way back to me, blinded by the light, yet relieved that I'd finally released us both from the awful journey.

In the end, she played her role perfectly. She mistreated me, so I did not give up finding my way home to my spirit. She fought for me by mistreating me and showing me that I needed to find a way to love myself without her. Without her, I don't think I could have kept up the fight for my love and light. She was now free to stop abusing me. And I was free to love her as my mommy. I freed us both that day from all the misery of denying ourselves the love that we spent our lives longing for.

She announced she was tired and ready for a nap. Unsteady on her feet, I took her arm and walked her down the bumpy sidewalk to her room. I remember her having to go to the bathroom. Every step from the bathroom to her bedroom felt so honest and timely. It felt like I was in a dream, and I could not handle the floor under my own feet. As I entered her tiny room, I noticed the picture of my daughters. I had also freed them that day by honoring me. I removed her shoes and helped her to bed, pulled the blankets up over her thin, frail body.

And I remember her saying, "I'm scared."

I answered, "Yes, I know you are afraid. Life is scary."

I placed my lips on her forehead.

I kissed her for the last time and said, "I love you, Mom."

"I love you too, sweetheart."

And she closed her eyes. I left that day with tears of joy. I rejoiced in the battle over loving her and being disappointed by her. And the resentment I felt toward myself for loving her was dead. I was free to love myself again. She was now free to move on.

I would never see her again. She passed away eleven months later, on August 12, 2020. I knew deep inside that it was the perfect planned date for her death. Relief swept over me, grateful I let her go one year before. Her diagnosis didn't matter because I knew she finally decided to let go. To let go of the fear of death. It was the destined day. In the end, she made it to light.

I miss her. She taught me so much about how little we need to exist. She taught me that our wants and desires keep us distracted from basic living. She was a simple woman who raised me simply because material items didn't mean anything to her. She never wanted those things. In the end, her children were her pride and joy, and she loved us the best way she knew how.

Human conditioning and society would have us believe that a mother should act and behave in a particular manner to be considered a good mother. The soul on its spiritual evolution here on Earth only evolves through relationships with other humans. Our relationships with our parents are always about the soul's spiritual evolution, not the social meanings of a mother or a father. The spiritual unraveling of the human experience is dreamy and mystical. Each ending brings me closer to my heart's desire for who I am. Each end brings me one step closer to the truth.

# Chapter 10

# The Ultimate Sacrifice

*"The more you know yourself, the more you forgive yourself."*
~Confucius

My next adventure came with a motorcycle journey across nine states with Rick and me on our Triumph 900 adventure bikes. Riding always brings me into the present moment, where I am looking straight into myself. The trip was planned before the death of mom yet perfect for grieving the loss. Both of my parents were gone. I was now able to see the purpose of my journey with my father.

After a couple of weeks of riding, Rick and I landed in Escalante, Utah because Rick had always wanted to hike in a slot canyon. We soon discovered some of the superb slots in this area. I remember standing in the hot desert sun, gazing downward, observing my blue trail tennies (sneakers). My body sweated in the heat, and my shoulders burned uncomfortably under the desert sun. The idea I had of a slot canyon was that it would wander among the red rocks. As far as my eye could see, only gray gravel and no red stone in sight. I felt like we were walking in a gravel pit. I became irritated that Rick and I may be lost walking back and forth looking for the slot in the canyon.

Soon my irritation turned into anger. When anger showed up, it usually meant I was resisting a shift coming up from within my body. Anger was my precursor to feeling something that I was afraid to feel. Tears began to well up in my eyes. This unknown, unseen energy pushed me. I could feel the emotions rising. There was no shade, no relief; we couldn't seem to find the slot in the canyon. I was worn out and tired of the hot sun.

"It's somewhere nearby, just a few more steps," Rick said. "I know it's over here."

I lashed out at him, spewing my anger towards him. As we wandered down the path to our left, Rick discovered the slot.

We walked for hours in the desert and finally entered the Red Rock's cocoon. The feeling of being in that three-foot-wide space with its twenty-foot-high stone walls was cool and comforting. Sunlight shone down from the opening overhead, lighting the path down the canyon. I was in awe of Mother Earth's womb and felt calmer and safer as we walked the mile-long red rock slot. I can remember running my hands across the smooth, swirling rock, sensing the energy of the stone. I stopped to rest, and I pressed my cheek against the coolness of the stone. Emotions swirled through every cell in my body, and I felt weak at my knees. Tears flowed down my face as I made my way to the end of the slot. I didn't know why I was crying or what I was feeling.

As mysteriously as we found the niche, it ended. I looked up and saw an almond-shaped opening, like a vagina announcing the end of the place. The energy rumbled from the depths of my subconscious. I leaned against Rick's chest, and I let it out, let it flow, let it go.

My subconscious revealed my broken heart. Those emotions ached deep inside my right groin, but my tears allowed me to let go of my father and the things he had done to me. I sensed this deep, old soul, karmic healing happening in this crack of the earth. As the energy released, I realized my father was the catalyst that sent me on my soul's karmic healing of separation from my Divinity. He had to break my heart with those sexual acts so I could begin my journey back to myself.

On that autumn day, being held by the only other man I have ever loved, I let go of the lock on my heart that kept me believing I was a terrible person who deserved suffering. Waves of emotion racked my body as I released the energetic ties to my sexual hell. Rick caught me as my knees buckled beneath me. I let him support me. Grief and sadness left my body as I allowed my husband to hold me in his arms, honoring me in my vulnerability while I let go of my broken heart, weeping as I entered into the depth of my love.

Those emotions of sadness and grief opened my heart a little more to see my Divinity. I let go of that tension I thought was protecting me. My shoulders fell forward, and my jaw released the anger I had contained for more than forty years.

In that moment of releasing my father, I still hadn't realized that I had been torturing myself with my perception of who I was. The thoughts kept me trapped in believing that it was not safe to be me, that it was too hard to be happy. My happiness turned into worry. All my energy had gone into protecting myself from joy. I had convinced myself that it wasn't safe to be happy.

It has taken me a long time to see that the only one violating me was me. When you don't know what you don't know, you don't know. I could say that I created this journey perfectly to see the true me. To be me is to be the light of my true nature. Some of us have to endure more pain than others before seeing how powerful we are. I'm not quite all the way there yet. My energy is so vital that my mind, body, and spirit can only attune to so much at one time. Each day I come into my body and my frequency a little bit at a time. If I allowed my entire spirit to enter my body, I would blow myself up.

I know this sounds dramatic, but the truth is life force energy (Kundalini) is so powerful and robust that it can cause a rush of heat that begins at the base of the spine and results in a spontaneous body spasm and confusion of the mind. Life force energy moves through each chakra at the rate we are supposed to individually evolve. Each of us is individual in our Kundalini awakening. For me, the spinning life force energy broke up the emotions, leaving my body shaking uncontrollably and spent from the powerful energetic release. Sometimes this can last for minutes, hours, or days. It's crucial to allow Spirit to enter the body at the rate the mind can absorb it.

We often don't know what it takes to release the karmic acts from lifetimes or even from this life until we go through a deep healing process. I was wide open after the slot canyon, allowing spirit to flow through me. I had no idea how being this wide-open would shift my entire karmic lineage.

## The Ultimate Sacrifice: Forgiving Myself

Walls of red rock surrounded me. I sat near the edge of the vast stone cathedral of Boynton Canyon in Sedona. The energy invited me to sit; I intuitively knew to cover my head with the yellow scarf I carry. I could feel the sun's warmth on my face and the heat from the rocks underneath me. As I turned my head and looked into the sun, I was drawn inward to that place inside that is warm and nurturing. The pull of the energy guided me toward my belly. I closed my eyes and drifted off, falling into a meditative state effortlessly. Colors swirled before me, and I felt a familiar presence. I settled into my sense of self. I heard the voice of spirit whispering *you are safe*. My mind tried to sort out what it meant to be safe. Safe on earth or secure in this body or safe from the past.

127

My mind relaxed, and I laid my body on the enormous red rock. Images began to appear before my mind's eye. Soon, a picture of myself as a man appeared. In the image, I was beating a woman. Suddenly I saw all of the horrible things I have done to women in my past lives. I saw myself as a man who had committed violent sexual acts on women. At that moment, I found forgiveness for what I had done. My heart opened, and I saw that I was the man who raped my mother. At that moment, I recognize that I am me, Denise, the little girl, I am my mom, and I am the wrong men. I stayed with those images of my lifetimes as a man who abused women. I stayed present to what I was witnessing. I saw my healing. My body was twisting, and I began to shake uncontrollably.

Then I heard the voice of spirit speak, *this is not the man you are today.* My husband was lying next to me. I had a death grip on his hand. During those healing times, I found his presence to be very grounding. He has an energy that protects me. Spirit went on to say *the man you are today is lying next to you. Kind, compassionate, generous, and loving.* I grabbed Rick a little tighter as that dark energy that I had been afraid of swooped in front of my third eye. As fast as that dark energy appeared, it disappeared. That was the energy that had me believing that I was a terrible person who didn't deserve love.

I have carried lifetimes of energies from the times I have been a male that committed horrible atrocities on humanity. I see now that my journey with dad was to untether my soul from lifetimes of abusing women. My spirit has always guided me to clear my past soul experiences as a man. I can see now that my journey with my dad is complete. I had to work through being unloved with my mother to know the truth of what I was hiding – lifetimes of horrible memories of torture. I faced my darkest shadow in Boynton Canyon.

I see it as balancing the polarities in me – the balancing of lifetimes of separation from the true me. So much of the time, I wanted to rid myself of the negativity. Today, I see it as balancing the truth in what I am willing to see. For without the darkness, there is no light. I freed my father and everyone who was ever connected to me emotionally from those horrible traumatic experiences that I believed were me.

If there's an antagonist in this story, the antagonist is me. I tortured myself by thinking that I was a horrible person. For so long, I couldn't let go of feeling like I was an awful person because I was afraid of what I might see. I was scared to face the horrible person I had been in so many lifetimes. Yet I was lost, and I knew it. But that loss was familiar. I knew it all too well. It took a tremendous amount of strength and courage to release the energy my body had contained for lifetimes.

Soon I developed compassion for my soul's journey. Understanding allowed me to forgive myself for my choices as a soul coming to this earth plane to clean up lifetimes of experiences. Here I began to sense the mind, the heart, the body in connection to God. And in those moments of presence, there's love.

Love doesn't always look like what our minds perceive it to be. In the center of the heart, where love resides, there's still sadness in the joy. There's anger in love. There's also nothingness in the beloved. That nothingness feels neutral. Soon you become bored with the void. Soon the mind wants to create drama. I couldn't see that I was living out the masculine part of myself, the mind, hiding my true identity. I was never able to fully surrender my femininity to my heart and my ability to express what I am feeling.

Letting go is a process. It's not a one-and-done event. It is a layering of letting go repeatedly, continually, each time to reach a new level of our Divinity. We get shown the next layer of our shit. It's all energy that wants to be released. The power trapped in our bodies from an emotional event is what we are removing. We are cleansing and clearing our old world and making room inside our bellies for the new world. Slowly the energy is revealing a new identity as a person. Gradually we return to our natural state of love.

# Chapter 11

# Self-Acceptance = Self-Love

*"You yourself, as much as anybody in the entire Universe,
deserve your love and affection."*
~Buddha

Rick and I rode our motorcycles over Cottonwood Pass in Colorado on my fifty-fifth birthday and set up camp among the aspens at Lotus Creek. The aspen trees with golden leaves shimmering in the wind hypnotizing me to go within. Drawn by their Divine nature, I felt relaxed in my body. My physical eyes were seeing the red rock backdrop joyfully, and the delicacy of the golden leaves made me feel happy. Experiencing this pleasure created excitement and an intense feeling of well-being.

The following day when I woke, I still felt drugged by love. Feeling playful, I sensed that Rick could feel it too. Tingling sensations and a buzzing frequency run through every cell of my body. Suddenly I was aware that I had no thoughts. We noticed that I was overly joyful. Everything seemed like a dream moving in slow motion, my body light and floaty. My mind was still and quiet. This strong desire to look into the sun pulled me toward my center, and instantly I went deeper into nothing. My chest expanded, my body relaxed, freedom flooded my brain, and I dropped back into that drugged-induced state of love.

We walked along the edge of the creek, the water trickling a magical tune. The rounded river rocks scattered far enough apart for us to walk our way up the creek's canyon. Each step was slow, methodically placed. My efforts were light and present as we made our way into the aspen forest. This state of presence felt surreal and Divine.

Rick laughed at me after asking ten times, "Are you sure you didn't spike my coffee?" We continued to walk in silence. No thoughts. No emotions. No drama. Only presence.

The sound of Rick's voice popped me out of my little bubble long enough to listen, only to sink back into my world of intense joy and love. The light streamed through the aspen's iridescent yellow leaves, blinding me, hypnotizing me back into a bliss state of relaxed ease. Time stood still as I wandered through the trees. Along the creek, the sunlight streamed through the trees and pulled me deeper into the love… and suddenly, I could not perceive Rick, even though I knew he was right beside me.

Startled that I could not see Rick, that familiar feeling of fear stung my gut. Gazing towards the clouded sky, I heard Spirit's voice, *"Come."* Suddenly my ego-mind thought I was being asked to leave this earth plane. "No, no, I can't go without Rick." I know now that I was being asked to let go, to surrender the soul and mind to my heart and spirit. As suddenly as Rick disappeared, he reappeared right next to me.

I have often reflected, "Did I miss an opportunity, or was that a taste of what is yet to come?" That was the day my spirit began the descent into my body. I was leaving my identity behind, ascending the ego-mind. The soul was leaving the mind and uniting with spirit in the middle of my chest.

I'm sure that day was Divinely planned, and I showed up. Surrounded by aspen trees, hundreds of miles from home, relaxed, on my birthday, a crescendo of energy all accumulated at the exact moment to bring me to a place of peace to hear the voice of spirit.

I hadn't fully understood what my teacher meant by ascension. I believed that you could leave this planet. I'm sure that's an option. I love this journey as a human being. But I know now what's happening. My soul had descended from my mind to be led by its new master, the heart. And as much as I wanted Rick to be there by my side, I can also see how I've identified with the idea that I can't go without him.

## Identities

As I transcended from the mind to the heart, I began thinking about identities. The soul is all about individuality and what role you play in other people's movies. Through the many years of healing work, meditation, yoga, and walking the forest, I have been able to identify specific identities. And in doing so, when those identities attempted to rear their heads in times of struggle, I named them or worked with them to release and to then allow my intuitive guidance from Spirit to be available rather than the ego.

As a professional mountain bike racer, if my legs weren't burning, it meant I wasn't trying hard enough. Life in general, if there wasn't drama, then I wasn't living. And if I wasn't making enough money, that meant I was a poor loser. At an early age, I took on the identity that it was my job to make others' lives better at the expense of my own life and well-being. When my daughters would come to me with their life struggles, I believed as a mother, I was the one that was supposed to fix it. Isn't that what mothers do? They make things better.

In my relationship with my mother, my identity was to be a good daughter. I did everything, from paying my mother's rent to boosting her up when she was depressed, making her laugh, bringing her chocolates, anything to make her life better.

In my relationship with my husband, I took care of all the finances because his inheritance gave me a good life. I've taken on the identity and the role of keeping track of the money to make it better for him. Never burdening him with the financial struggles, just fixing it and making it better. My identity as a wife has been not to complain and make him happy by doing whatever it takes, not to burden him.

Every time my brother comes to me, I had great advice on what he should do to get what he wants out of life. I constantly propped him up and made him feel better so his life could be better. As a grandmother, I took on the identity to make everything fun and playful, giving my grandchildren all the things that I didn't have and didn't give my children. With my niece, I took on the identity of being the female role model in her life because she didn't have a mother. I tried to make up for the mother that she didn't have.

As for my father, I took on the identity of making it okay for what he did to me. When he asked for forgiveness, I told him that it was okay. "Dad, you played your role in my life perfectly." All so that he could feel better.

You see, there's a gap between the old self which is moving through the soul. The soul contains the ancient world of memories. All those ego identities and roles I played are wife, mother, daughter, father, and son. Ego integration meant losing the uniqueness of all those lifetimes of human roles that I played that left me feeling wrong. This new world, this spirit of the heart, dis-identified with the past or the future. The New World's frequency is love, and love is neutral. The heart is where we experience non-attachment.

## Self-Love

As I continually reached a new level of myself (and each time I landed in this place of self-love that lasted for a few months at a time), I felt safe, nurtured, and open. Self-love is a place of neutrality, but not being in the drama can be boring to the mind. I have trained my mind to behave by coming into the lower belly, where I locate the place of peace that connects me with the essence of what I am: joy, love, and happiness. Spirit. How often have I reached the top of the spiral or the mountain and been on this high? Because I am human, with every mountain climb, there's a descent.

Descending the hill from this new level of self-awareness started with happiness and joy. The drop brought me into this new refreshing sense of what I am. I am a spiritual being having a human experience. And this new sense of self-love became the new norm. Soon I found the newness wore off, and this is when my mind gets bored. Then I search for the next mountain to climb. I start thinking and believing I need to be doing something, not realizing the most important thing for me to do, if I were to do anything in this world, is do nothing and just be.

Sit and be in the frequency of the Divine, which is love. The sense of boredom is part of the transformation of the journey. It seems so profound that all life is a journey back to the heart and those feel-good feelings, only to find the mind getting bored with those feel-good feelings. Slowly that euphoric state becomes my new norm, yet I'm unable to see how far I've come each time. The new standard begins a new journey with more awareness, only to find I'm asking the age-old question: Is this it?

Self-love isn't just about feeling love in my heart. It's about listening to our innermost beings and honoring what we hear. It's about receiving the support of the Earth energy that awakens our life forces. The heart needs this physical body to express itself as the light and the power of love.

I thought self-love was all about living from the heart's space and creating that yumminess inside me. It's *that* and more. Listening to the gentle nudging of knowing and responding to those nudges is how the soul communicates with the spirit in me.

Coming into my body is foreign and confusing. It's hard to hear my body when my mind chatters and creates distractions that make it hard to see what is right in front of me. It's foreign to feel the high vibration of love. Maybe this is why it's so hard to accept love. When I fight this frequency of the yumminess of love, it can become overwhelmingly uncomfortable, causing dis-ease in my body.

## The Body

In January 2020, I found out that my gut was inflamed and not functioning at its optimal capacity for health. My hyper-vigilance – a direct response to overthinking – created stress in the body and made me unable to listen to my body. My yoga teacher said, "Your gut brain is the central brain – healthy gut-brain equals healthy mind-brain equals healthy heart-brain." I have since chosen to eat cleaner than I already did to stop punishing my body – the home of my soul. The constant ruminating thoughts of my mind created a toxic environment for my gut.

Listening to my ego-mind and believing that I was my thoughts had me abandoning my body and soul. My gut is where my emotions create feelings. And what I've learned is that it is hard for me to understand and feel my feelings. Each time I deny my feelings, I'm abandoning the spirit. Those feel-good feelings are intense at first for me, and I want to run back to my pain (my mind). Back to my emotional story and bypass the feelings my body is trying to get me to feel.

As a way to abandon my feelings, I'll either eat something I'm not supposed to eat or do something dangerous on my bicycle or my motorcycle, causing my body pain. I believe that accidents are not accidents; our bodies get us to stop and feel something that is ready to leave if we allow it. Pain is an indicator that something needs to be addressed.

Being in my body meant I had to feel the love that was present in me. Staying current with what I feel is how I don't abandon myself any longer. To feel self-love and express self-love is part of listening to my body. Every pain is an expression of a thought that is ready to be addressed. Pain or disease in the body is the body's way of communicating with us.

Our body is the messenger of the soul. Spirit speaks to us by reflecting into the body the truth of what we are. Spirit only speaks positively. It is the ego-mind that can be harmful, making it hard to hear the voice of the spirit. When we experience dis-ease, it comes from listening and believing our negative thoughts. The disconnection of the soul and the spirit is the dis-ease in the body.

Either way, good sensations or not-so-good sensations are feelings. And when we acknowledge and address physical pain by feeling into the pain, this is an act of self-love. Self-love is showing up for myself through the good and the bad by feeling whatever I am feeling, because without the sensations and the feelings in my body, I am numb. I float outside of myself in an endless loop of thoughts. The circle of ideas creates an identity that makes pain and suffering.

The ability to sit in the frequency of the yumminess of my self-generated love can be foreign, strange, and overwhelmingly uncomfortable. I disciplined my ego-mind to trust in the fearlessness of the unification of the soul and the spirit.

## Fearlessly Navigating My Heart

I stepped out my front door and began to jog down the tree-lined drive to the entrance of the forest. I noticed the quail scurrying through the brush. The doves rippled through the air, safely landing on an oak branch. For some months, this raven has been screeching, trying to get my attention. Today only silence as the shiny blackbird soars overhead. I began to jog faster, noticing the firmness of the earth beneath my feet. My breathing became labored as I warmed up.

Each tree acknowledged me, and I smiled openly. The fir trees' lime green needles invited me to feel the newness of their growth. The tenderness of the branches reminded me to nurture this new place I have entered on my journey. This love from the trees is an example of how Spirit always smiles back at me.

Suddenly, sticks snapped. A mama bear stood at the base of a tree, staring right at me. Her cub hid high up in the tree, looking down at me. My belly started, but it was not scary. I noticed I'm not afraid. I don't feel fearful meeting this wild bear and her baby. I turned around, gave her space, and made my way back home.

As I continued to run, I felt courageous and strong and tingly. A spontaneous exhalation rose through me, and a weight lifted. Chills run down my spine as I raised my arms to the sky in receptivity. The image of the locked-in memories left my body as I simultaneously allowed myself to feel the self-generated energy of the love happening inside of my body.

I could feel the mama bear's motherly energy, and I found myself playfully roaring, laughing, and smiling. My sense was another layer of my ego identity that lived in pain and suffering had left me. The feeling of sadness arose, aching my bones. I took a few deep breaths, exhaling long and slow. I allowed the emotion to arise unattached to the story that flashes before my eyes. Another layer healed.

The wise part of me (intuition) knew that it was time to feel everything, not just the pain but the love. My belly contracted, not wanting to feel. Spirit spoke to me, *Relax, and allow me to guide you. Feel it and let it flow.* I breathed my way through this overwhelming sadness that kept me angry at my ego-mind.

I stayed present with the love in my heart and spirit simultaneously as my soul let go of the ego-mind. I helped the soul realize that it was now the master of the mind. I know now that I am not my thoughts and what I think is not me. My soul united with Spirit in the center of my body. Spirit acknowledged my soul's journey and thanked my soul by apologizing for the arduous journey and separation. The soul and spirit were happy and playfully united after a long break from the heart frequency.

I finished my run feeling gratitude for all that I saw. I felt Spirit in the trees, the plants, and the birds. I know that I am the mind-body-soul-spirit guiding me through this Earth journey.

There was no thought when I was out in nature, only me. My inner world feels surreal. Freedom from controlling thoughts. I enjoyed my own company as I wandered in the forest, gazing inside, and connecting with this body. Everything looking back at me was kind. It was as if the woods had always been waiting for me.

The soul integrated with spirit creating the new world. The personality of my soul still exists as strength, courage, a strong will, a powerful mind, and a willingness to succeed. Spirit is playful, funny, joyful, and happy. As Soul and Spirit integrate, I could see more clearly what I am.

The bear came and showed me that I have the strength to navigate these two worlds. I can go out in the external world of everyday life experiences and still know what I am. I have the power to hold the capacity of my heart of love and bring this high-frequency to the external world. The bear showed me that I dared to be the love in a world that is suffering. The bear showed me that I am protected, and it's safe to be guided by Spirit.

Today I recognize that when my mind is angry, it's just my ego wanting to create drama. Spirit is always happily ready to play and have fun. My awareness is acute, and I don't stay with negative thoughts for very long. Sure, I go there every once in a while, but it feels icky to be negative.

To be free to live means knowing I no longer have to suffer to fit into society. I have the freedom to be happy no matter what happens in the world. I am free to be the full expression of my spirit, happy, joyful, and playful. The most important lesson is knowing I have the choice to listen to my heart.

# Chapter 12

# This is It!

*"My religion consists of a humble admiration of the illimitable superior spirit who reveals himself in the slight details we are able to perceive with our frail and feeble mind."*
~Albert Einstein

I know it's time to step into my sense of self – the Goddess of Infinite Light. The truth is that I am loved. I am good and there's nothing more for me to do. I can hear my heart telling my body to relax and receive and rejoice in this truth. My ego-mind tries to rush back to the past to see if I have cleaned it all up. I'm finding that the only way to have peace is to surrender and trust that I have done enough to clean up the past. It's time to trust in my relationship with Spirit.

I've come a long way. I quietly ask my ego-mind to take a break from judging everything that it sees. No need to have an opinion about a simple blade of grass. I tune into my heart, and there's a frequency that I feel all around me. That frequency, when I'm present in the moment, is how I'm able to see all the same things without a thought of what I am seeing. In the stillness of my heart, I get to be me. Daily I get to choose the old world of the ego-mind or the new world in my belly where the spirit is now guiding my heart.

All those experiences with my parents were traumatic; it was my evolution of the soul. I guess what I'm trying to say here is that the karma from those experiences of being abused and abandoned became my dharma. Fighting the lies within the mind is what kept me on the path of self-realization. I've learned that the mind's job is to preserve our isolation and the ego-mind is designed to protect our identities.

I didn't know that my mind wasn't me. You see, I had to become entrapped because it was the vehicle to become untrapped. My evolution was and is the journey of this life, all created by me to become connected. The disconnection (the ego-mind) is the journey of the human experience (the soul) back to connection (Spirit). Exactly where we started. When I look at all the experiences that I planned for myself, I can now see the purpose of it all.

My karma was to experience being abandoned and unloved. The experience of abandonment has brought me to my dharma, my intention to be connected in the world. My disconnection from my experience is profound. Abandonment gave me the will to fight for myself.

Without disconnection, would I have fought for my connection? Probably not. I would have had the perfect parents and would not have seen that I was disconnected. I needed to be the victim of my parents to begin my journey of being connected. The mind would have been happy with the perfect parents in an ideal life, whatever that means. That wasn't the journey I chose. That wasn't the evolution I decided. The knowledge lies deep in all of us, and it never leaves us. It's always there observing, making sure that we don't get too far off-track. That presence of knowing of the connectedness of Spirit never left me and has always been guiding me.

## The Journey of Finding Connection

Over the past ten years, beautiful human beings have shown up to reflect my actual state of being. I was too blind to see or hear the loving kindness they showed me, their positive talk, their love. I was so attached to the old identity, I could not see the love that they were reflecting back to me. I was always searching for validation that I was okay. Once validated, I'd ignore the confirmation. That's how attached to the perception of myself I had become. I couldn't see that my reality was a lie and an illusion. All that time, it was sitting right in front of me. I was stuck in my suffering, blinded by my darkness of negativity.

Each time I would get a glimpse of that connectedness, I would convince myself that this wasn't it. It couldn't be that simple. Love feels strange to the ego-mind, so odd that it is unable to grasp what it is experiencing. There has to be more to it than all this quietness. This isn't it. Down the spiral, my ego convinced me once again that the experience of love and connectedness wasn't real.

As long as I identified as the abandoned, abused child, I was somebody, and I kept creating that same somebody over and over again.

The ego-mind believes that good feelings come from the money in the bank, the fancy car we drive, or the beautiful home we own. What we're really searching for is that feeling of connectedness that comes from living from the heart. When you live from the heart, you can be in the world without being identified by the mind.

Every shitty experience involving another human being was just an act in a movie to show me what identity I'd been playing, just like every positive human experience showed me the goodness of my humanness. Part of our human nature is that we need polarity to see our state.

Today I understand that the nature of suffering is me identifying as somebody. When I think of myself as nobody, I'm not my body, I'm not my thoughts, I'm not my emotions. When I'm in nature, I find myself tuned in to what is around me, and I'm not caught up in my separateness. Nature has helped me find my place in my heart where I feel. In this connected state, I'm loved and whole and connected, but most of all, I'm free of any identity.

Right now, there is a level of acceptance for it all. I know now that I am not an abandoned, abused child or a horrible person. In those moments of contentedness, I see the spirit in all living things, the essence of each tree's character, and its stance. The nature of me is the frequency of love that connects me to all living things.

This is it – stillness and being connected to my inner world by an inner universe. Nature shows me that I am love, that I am loved, and that I am safe, and I am free to be. Nature brings me into the present moment. That connectedness found in the stillness of my heart has freed me from the identity of the abandoned, abused child.

To embody Love as Spirit is the journey to save humanity. I have come to know that Spirit resides in my core and Soul surrounds the Spirit through what is known as the Aura. The resonance of love, joy and happiness reflects the soul, and this becomes the new experience – life as co-creation. I now know Soul is being guided by Spirit. This is the "we" I have come to know as The One.

Today Denise has taken her own experiences with healing emotionally, physically, and spiritually and created the Your Energy Awakening System (Discover-Activate-Illuminate), which led her to create Spirit Vision Quest. Vision Quests are held on her private ranch in Northern California where she resides with her husband Rick. Denise believes that the spirit in nature will ignite the light of your true nature. Which is LOVE. Denise can be contacted at: denise@yourenergyawkening.com.